Jousts and Tournaments

Charny and the Rules for
Chivalric Sport in Fourteenth-Century France

Steven Muhlberger

Jousts and Tournaments:
Charny and the Rules for Chivalric Sport in Fourteenth-Century France

Original material © 2002 Steven Muhlberger
Charny French edition © 1977 Michael Anthony Taylor
ISBN: 1-891448-28-5

Design by Brian R. Price
Printed in Thailand

Published in the United States by
The Chivalry Bookshelf
Union City, California, 94587
tel. 866.268.1495 (US)
fax 978.418.4774
http://www.chivalrybookshelf.com

Authors
   Charny, Geoffroi de (fl. 1356)
   Muhlberger, Steven (1950-)
   Taylor, Michael Anthony (19xx-)

Library of Congress Cataloging-in-Publication Data
Charny, Geoffroi de (fl. 1356)
[Demands pour la joute, le tournoi, et la guere. English & French]
Jousts and tournaments : Charny and the rules for chivalric sport in fourteenth-century France / [translated with a commentary by] Steven Muhlberger.
    p. cm.
Includes bibliographical references (p.   ).
ISBN 1-891448-28-5
1. Tournaments, Medieval--History. 2. Military art and science--History--Medieval, 500-1500. 3. Knights and knighthood--History. I. Muhlberger, Steven. II. Title.
CR4553.C48 2003
394'.7'09440902--dc21
                              2002156505

Neither the authors, editors, or publisher accepts any responsibility for the use or misuse of information contained in this book.

CONTENTS

Acknowledgments..vi
Illustration credits..ix
Notes about the Abbreviations & Bibliography........................x
Introduction..1

Part I
Exploring Chivalric Sport

1. Jousting and Jousters..19
2. Horses and Horsemen..37
3. The Jousting Scene — some incautious speculation....................53
4. The Tourney..61
5. Knights and Debaters..85

Part II
Charny's Questions on the Joust and the Tourney

Text (Michael A. Taylor edition) and Translation................96
Bibliography..144

Ruta

Acknowledgments

This project pounced on me when I thought I was working on something else. Many people deserve thanks for helping me to get a grip on it.

Brian Price alerted me to the existence of Charny's *Questions*, when he published Daryle Pompeo's translation in *Chronique: The Journal of Chivalry*. When I belatedly took a serious interest in the *Questions*, he provided me with a variety of useful material and lots of encouragement. He also made available the Tournament Companies e-mail list at Topica.com for a discussion of these questions with an interested audience. Michael Taylor's edition of the *Questions* was my starting point. I thank him for allowing excerpts from his work to be reprinted here.

While translating the *Questions* I consulted as widely as I could on various problems I found in the text. Daryle Pompeo's translation and advice were very helpful in the initial phases. As I progressed, Elizabeth Z. Bennett, Reed Thomas, and especially Florence Brémond were generous with their time and suggestions. Thanks to them, there are many fewer errors in the translation than there might be.

Late in the project, I was alerted to the existence of Sicily Herald's treatise on tournaments by Torsten Hiltmann of the Technischen Universität Dresden and the École Pratique des Hautes Études Paris; he and Klaus Oschema of the same institutions generously provided me with copies of this difficult to find text. My thanks to them for making possible comparisons between Charny and Sicily Herald. Suzanne Kocher of the University of Louisiana at Lafayette, Philip Bennett of the University of Edinburgh, Christos Nüssli and John Mackinnon kindly helped me interpret the language of Sicily Herald.

During the month of October, 2001, I had the privilege of leading a discussion of Charny's *Questions* on Brian Price's Tournament Companies list, which is usually devoted to the re-enactment of medieval deeds of arms. Dozens of re-enactors, creative anachronists, jousters, and scholars took part. However much they may have learned from that discussion, I learned more, simply because they took the material seriously and energetically engaged with it and with me. Any scholar knows that an interested and intelligent audience is a most valuable resource. Their reactions, arguments, and ideas provide what you can't or haven't come up with yourself, and their enthusiasm is the stimulant you need when you wonder if the subject is worth your effort. My profound gratitude to everyone who contributed to that creative and enjoyable month.

I am extremely grateful to two others who have been willing to talk with me about the *Questions*. Will McLean has been studying deeds of arms for much longer than I have, and he has been very generous in sharing his knowledge of the sources, in criticizing my interpretations, and providing alternatives to them. I am looking forward to his reaction to this book, to which he has contributed a great deal. My wife, Ruta Muhlberger, has also been an intelligent and critical reader and audience. Her sympathetic appreciation of my work means more than all the rest put together.

Thanks as well to the following: Nipissing University for general scholarly support; Susan Randle of the Nipissing University Interlibrary Loan Department; Craig Taylor of the University of York for bibliographic suggestions; the anonymous readers of the manuscript for many useful comments; the Knights of Valour of Waterford, Ontario, for showing me jousting first hand; and various friends and members of the Society for Creative Anachronism who have paid me the compliment of being interested in this project.

Illustrations

Cover: BL. MS Add. 12228, courtesy the Trustees of the British Library.

Figure 1, p. xii: FR2813-394, courtesy Bibliothèque Nationale de France.

Figure 2, p. 18: Manesse Codex, fol. 52r., courtesy Universtätsbibliothek Heidelberg.

Figure 3, p. 36: Manesse Codex, fol. 17r., courtesy Universtätsbibliothek Heidelberg.

Figure 4, p. 52: Manesse Codex, fol. 18r., courtesy Universtätsbibliothek Heidelberg.

Figure 5, p. 84: Manesse Codex, fol. 61v., courtesy Universtätsbibliothek Heidelberg.

Figure 6, p. 92: Manesse Codex, fol. 192v., courtesy Universtätsbibliothek Heidelberg.

Abbreviations for the Notes and Bibliography

Charny's *Questions Concerning the Joust, Tournaments, and War* are broken into the three sections indicated by the title. In this book I refer to individual questions by the section (J, T, or W) and by number. Thus, T14 = question 14 concerning tournaments. The full text of Charny's questions on jousting and tourneying and questions 1, 3, 4, and 5 on war can be found in Part II of this book, with an accompanying English translation. The text is taken from Michael Taylor's edition in his unpublished Ph.D. dissertation, University of North Carolina, 1977. My thanks to him for allowing excerpts from his edition to be included here. The translation is mine.

The translations from Froissart's *Chronicles* are based on Thomas Johnes' nineteenth-century version, which in some case have been corrected or modified to better conform to contemporary English usage.

Barber and Barker

Barber, Richard and Juliet Barker. *Tournaments: Jousts, chivalry and pageants in the Middle Ages.* Woodbridge: Boydell Press, 1989.

Barker

Barker, Juliet R.V. *The Tournament in England, 1100-1400.* Woodbridge: Boydell Press, 1986.

Fleckenstein

Fleckenstein, Josef, ed. *Das ritterliche Turnier im Mittelalter: Beiträge zu einer vergleichenden Formen- und Verhaltensgeschichte des Rittertums.* Göttingen: Vandenhoeck & Ruprecht, 1985.

Froissart

Froissart, Jean. *Oeuvres: Chroniques.* Edited by Kervyn de Lettenhove. 25 vols. in 26. Reprint edition. Osnabrück: Biblio Verlag, 1967.

Johnes

Froissart, Sir John. *Chronicles of England, France, Spain and the Adjoining Countries...* Translated by Thomas Johnes. 2 vols. London: Bohn, 1869.

René

King René's Tournament Book: René d'Anjou, Traictié de la forme et devis d'ung tournoy. Translated by Elizabeth Bennett. N.p., 1992. Online: http://www.princeton.edu/~ezb/rene/renehome.html

> For the French text of René I have used the version in Francis Henry Cripps-Day. *The History of the Tournament in England and France.* London: Bernard Quaritch, 1918. Appendix VIII.

Michael Anthony Taylor

Taylor, Michael Anthony, ed. "A Critical Edition of Geoffroy de Charny's 'Livre Charny' and the 'Demandes pour la joute, les tournois, et la guerre.'" Unpublished Ph.D. dissertation, University of North Carolina, 1977.

U.P.

University Press

Fig. 1: *Companions of the Order of the Star*...FR 2813-394, courtesy Bibliothèque Nationale de France.

Steven Muhlberger

INTRODUCTION

Everyone knows that the knights of the Middle Ages amused themselves in jousts and tournaments. It is widely understood how important these sports were as practical and symbolic exercises in chivalry. Yet readers interested in factual descriptions of how such games were played are often frustrated by how little is known about the rules, the conventions, the tactics and the forms of combat. This obscurity is not due to a lack of scholarly effort. The history of chivalric sport has been the subject of research and discussion for centuries. Doubt and ignorance persist because most medieval depictions of tournaments, jousts and other formal deeds of arms are fictional or highly colored literary accounts. Detailed regulations governing these activities and manuals prescribing how they should be organized were not committed to writing before second half of the fifteenth century. Such documents hardly exhaust our curiosity even about the sports of that later time; but for earlier periods, the situation is much worse, because existing descriptions are celebrations of chivalry, not matter-of-fact records. Centuries of practice are tantalizingly beyond our grasp.

This book is an exploration of an exceptional, early text – one dating from the mid-fourteenth century – which was devoted not to commemorating great formal deeds of arms, but to discussing the practical problems that might arise in connection with the sports of a martial aristocracy. It is a text that presents us with many difficulties, but which nevertheless gives us a unique and down-to-earth perspective on the actual behavior of knights taking part in organized, ostensibly friendly competitions.

About the year 1350, Geoffroi de Charny, a veteran French knight, composed a work called *Questions Concerning the Joust, Tournaments, and War* (*Les Demandes pour la joute, les tournois et la guerre*). The *Questions* were written with a specific audience in mind: "the high and mighty prince of the Knights of Our Lady of the Noble House. . .and the knights of our noble company."[1] That prince was John II, King of France; the noble company was the king's short-lived chivalric order, usually called the Order of the Star, which was formally launched, after long consideration, in 1352, to revitalize the practice of chivalry in his realm.[2] Charny was closely associated with King John in this period, and scholars believe that to aid the king in his aims, Charny wrote not only the *Questions*, but also two treatises on chivalry: one in verse, the *Livre Charny* or *Book of Charny*,[3] and one in prose, the *Livre de la chevalerie* or *Book of Chivalry*.[4] The treatises were meant to evoke the warrior's way of life, and encourage nobles to rededicate themselves to it. The *Questions* were meant as a practical guide to legal issues that might arise between "strenuous" or active knights while using arms, on the battlefield or on the tourney field. The *Questions*, therefore, are part of a unique body of writings defining and describing chivalry as Charny saw it.[5]

To anyone who wants to understand what "chivalry" meant in mid-fourteenth century France, Charny's writings have considerable importance. They presumably reflect not only his own extensive military experience but also the perceptions of the royal court whose patronage he enjoyed. Even before he began to write, Charny's military career had been a long one, going back to 1337, when he first served in Gascony under the Constable of France at the start of the Hundred Years War. He fought in several campaigns against the English and in a crusade against the Turks in Anatolia. He participated in a number of sieges and in a pitched battle at Morlaix in 1342, where he was captured and held for ransom. The most famous story associated with him concerns his attempt, in December of 1349, to recapture Calais for France by bribing a Lombard captain in the English garrison, a coup frustrated when the Lombard revealed his own treachery to Edward III. The English king was waiting with a picked company to surprise Charny's force when they were admitted to Calais, late one night, by the now-repentant traitor. Some of the French fled, but Charny himself was taken a second time and spent the year 1350 and part of 1351 in England.[6]

Despite the two major setbacks and resulting captivities that stand out in any brief summary of his early career, Charny must have appeared at mid-century as a bold and noteworthy warrior. He had clearly risen by the exercise of his personal talents. Charny was noble enough to be knighted early in life, but he held no major fief that by itself would make him a prominent warrior or political figure. Nevertheless, as early as Morlaix he was being given major responsibilities, and in 1348 he was added to the royal council in response to demands that King Philip VI find more worthy councilors to advise him about the conduct of the war. His second captivity did not harm his reputation in any way. The new king, John II, contributed to his ransom. Upon his return, John put him to work in a variety of responsible positions, most notably as the "Captain General of the Wars of Picardy and the Frontiers of Normandy," in other words, overall commander of the northern frontier in the ongoing war against England. The highest mark of royal esteem was Charny's designation as keeper of the Oriflamme, the royal battle banner, which was regarded as a sacred relic and brought out only for the most important royal campaigns. Charny bore the Oriflamme in the campaign of 1356 and was killed defending it at Poitiers in September of that year.[7]

This short summary of Charny's career shows him to be a natural choice to be a chief royal advisor when the king was reorganizing France for war, in part through his launching of the Order of the Star. A "strenuous knight" by any measure, he had the qualities that would give weight to his opinions when he spoke about war and chivalry. Charny's writings were produced in a very active time in his life, in the early 1350s, when he both enjoyed royal favor and was engaged in the king's business, on campaign, in the council, and on diplomatic missions. In those years he must have seemed to be a key figure at the royal court, a living symbol of King John's determination to make war more effectively than his unsuccessful father.

Recently, interest in Charny has been aroused by the publication of a fine new edition and translation of the *Book of Chivalry* by Kaeuper and Kennedy. Charny has been revealed as a man of considerable persuasive powers, who felt it his duty to encourage the practice of the military virtues. Charny's eloquence, as demonstrated in the *Book of Chivalry*, allows the reader an imaginative insight into the world of knights and their values and, perhaps best of all, the flavor of their discussions, which were almost never recorded.

Questions Concerning the Joust, Tournaments, and War ought to give us similar insight into the world of chivalric effort and chivalric reflection. Yet this work has received very little attention, even from the historians of the tournament, to whom it might especially seem to appeal, given the lack of documentation for the rules of such activities.[8] Any reader looking at the *Questions* will soon realize why this is the case. Charny's puzzles, whether they concern all-out war or more friendly martial activities, are offered up without any answers, a fact universally lamented by those who read them. If we had those answers, our knowledge of war, jousting (a one-on-one competition) and tourneying (a contest between teams) in the early fourteenth century would be vastly greater.

Yet the more one studies the *Questions*, the less confident one becomes that all of them could be unambiguously answered even in the 1350s. Some of the *Questions* are philosophical and posed in such a way as to guarantee debate. For instance, question 90 on war asks simply, "Which do you prefer, intelligence or prowess (*ou sen ou prouuesce*)?" Question 91 likewise looks for an exchange of views:

> Which would you prefer: that you were held of no account in regard to deeds of arms of war, but in all deeds of arms of peace [i.e. jousts and tournaments] where you have been or ever will be present you would have taken the day or would have the prize; or, rather, that in all deeds of arms of war where you have been or will be present you have been and will be regarded as having done the best, without any other prize, and in deeds of arms of peace you were held of no account?[9]

Other cases, the majority of the *Questions*, do seek to draw from the audience a legal definition or a ruling on a dispute. Charny many times asks how a matter will be judged "according to the law of arms." But he is well aware that the law of arms was open to interpretation. Charny often ends a question with "What do you say?" In question 13 on the joust, he asks, "Should the squire win the horse? What do you say? What might others think?" A number of the war questions, after setting out the facts, end with the statement "Many good arguments are put forward about it on one side or the other," evoking not just disagreement, but the fluidity of the "law of arms."

To understand the *Questions* better, we can look at their original context, especially at the Order of the Star, their intended audience. The Order, although it seems to have met only once, in January of 1352, was a serious and ambitious effort by King John II to renew the chivalry of France in a period when its poor performance in war had left it open to criticism. The Order was meant, according to a surviving royal letter of election to an unknown member, to include eventually 500 knights. There were apparently to be three types of members: princes, that is great lords; bannerets, that is knights (some, perhaps, of baronial status) who led major retinues and who were capable of holding significant commands; and bachelors, knights whose rank was not as exalted as the other two, but who were still considerable lords. It has been estimated that there were no more than 4000 strenuous knights in all of France at this time, and perhaps considerably fewer. Had the Order ever reached its projected size, it might have included a fifth of France's fighting chivalry, and, if John had so chosen, all of the bannerets, barons, and greater lords of the realm, with room left over for a good number of bachelors. Such an Order was meant to reshape not only the practice of chivalry, but also the relationship between the monarch and the leading warriors of the kingdom.[10]

It was the king's intention that the entire Order would gather annually at the Noble House, a lavish complex to be built at the royal residence of Saint-Ouen near Paris. It was here that feasts, religious celebrations, and a "full court" concerned with chivalric affairs were to take place. According to the chronicler Jean le Bel,

> ... there each of the companions was to recount all of the adventures, the shameful as well as the glorious, which had come to him in the time since he had been in the noble court. And the king was to establish two or three clerks who were to listen to all these adventures and put them in a book, so that they might be reported there before the companions, by which one could know the most valorous and honor those who best deserved it.[11]

The reporting of deeds was connected to the judging of them. According to the royal letter of election, nine members of the Order — three princes, three bannerets, and three bachelors — would be selected to sit at the Table of Honor during the yearly banquet, based on their performance in war. It is not specified in the letter who made this choice, but surely the companions had a role in choosing or acclaiming them; Jean le Bel states "no one could enter this into this Company if he did not have the consent of the king and the greater part of the companions present."[12] The royal letter says that the Prince [i.e., King John] and his *conseil* would judge how a knight who had behaved disgracefully should be punished. Logically, the "council" referred to would be the member knights of the Order, or perhaps some subset of them. Taken together, these bits of information show the annual gathering of the Order as a glittering *parlement* — deliberative assembly — of the leading chivalry of France, encouraging and rewarding warlike valor and punishing dereliction of duty.

This same assembly was uniquely qualified to hear and judge the cases found in Charny's *Questions*. To achieve the reform purpose of the Order, King John would have filled it with established leaders of chivalric society and promising younger knights. These warriors would have had reason to believe they knew a thing or two about knightly sport and the proper conduct of war. They were men who quite naturally thought of themselves as judges. All must have been *seigneurs*, lords of people and of lands, with courts of their own. And it was men such as they who were naturally called upon to discuss problems in the law of arms when they arose.

What was this "law of arms?"

Decades ago, Maurice Keen showed that in the later Middle Ages there was a such a law, which, if it was not codified, was the subject of much discussion and practical consequence, and applied to the behavior of "men-at-arms" — competent, fully-equipped warriors of standing.[13] The mid-fourteenth century was a period when that law and the courts that dealt with it were becoming more formalized all over Europe, but especially in England and France. The first phase of the Hundred Years War drove institutional development by increasing the number of cases that fell under the law of arms. The 1340s seems to have been the period when the English constable's court gained a new prominence and a more permanent jurisdiction over the law of arms; a body of documents about such cases before this court has survived. In France, at about the same time, many cases judged in the first instance by courts using the law of arms were finding their way, through appeals, to the Parlement of Paris, in the archives of which they can be found.¹⁴ Other surviving evidence for the content of the law of arms include learned treatises produced in vernacular languages (which shows a desire for a wider, lay audience). In 1387 the clerical lawyer Honoré Bouvet (also called Bonet) wrote *The Tree of Battles (L'Arbre des Batailles)*, a work that put into more accessible French many of the doctrines of Roman law applicable to matters arising out of war. Christine de Pizan's *The Book of Deeds of Arms and of Chivalry (Livre des Fayes d'Armes et de Chevalerie)* of 1410, which draws quite a bit of material from Bouvet, was a later attempt to popularize certain views of the "office" of chivalry and the laws of war.¹⁵

Charny's *Questions* must be seen as part of the fourteenth-century definition and formalization of that law; in fact, it is one of the earliest relevant documents. If the law of arms was now sometimes enforced by higher courts, in which professional lawyers had their place, it was based as much, if not more, on the customs of practical warriors than on the doctrines of university-trained experts like Bouvet.¹⁶ Judges ruling on the law of arms, at least in the first instance, were men holding military authority, such as commanders of garrisons, marshals and constables of major hosts, and lieutenants of provinces — in other words, they were knights, especially bannerets and "princes." These judges were often in the position of ruling on disputes on the spot, in summary procedures where disputants and witnesses were present and the case needed to be disposed of quickly. Any complexities that might arise would quite naturally be referred to other experienced and trusted men-at-arms — to "knights and squires of good reputation" (*chivalers et esquiers de valu*) as they were called in one arbitrated dispute of 1359.¹⁷

We can visualize a discussion of Charny's Questions in the assembly of the Order of the Star as a sincere effort to collect precedents and perhaps to legislate on difficult problems. Certainly John was an energetic legislator on military matters: at the same time that he was putting the finishing touches on his plans for the Order, he issued a "regulation for warriors" in which he defined military pay, equipment, and organization, in an effort to extend his control over the war-making capacity of the kingdom.[18] It is, however, probably more likely that the *Questions* had another goal, one not necessarily inconsistent with the first. We know that neither the king nor Charny was satisfied with the recent military performance of their fellow knights – the disaster of Crécy was only a few years past — and each was moved to do something about it. In the case of Charny, this led him to write two lengthy treatises to encourage his knightly fellows to take their martial duties more seriously; as he said repeatedly "he who does more is of greater worth." In the *Book of Chivalry* a desire to improve his fellows was joined to a subtle and respectful way of drawing his audience into his concerns. There, Charny avoided ranting or berating his readers — except when it came to discussing the indecencies of modern fashion. Rather, he reminded them of the worthiness of the martial way of life, and encouraged them to live up to its best traditions. If he implied that there were slackers among the chivalry of France, Charny never made the rhetorical mistake of telling his readers that they were slackers. One can see any discussion of the Questions, then, as being as a way of engaging his knightly peers in the effort to ascertain and reform existing practice. Debate on these issues would surely have revealed large differences of opinion and shaken up participants who had been previously certain that their opinions were shared by all good men-at-arms. If decisions were reached, well and good; at the very least debate would have honed the legal and analytical skills of the participants, and made them think seriously about things they had taken for granted.

It is easy to understand why Charny and his royal patron would wish leading knights to be well versed in the law of arms as it related to war. It is a little more difficult, perhaps, for a modern reader to comprehend why jousts and tournaments would be included in Charny's *Questions*. In fact, neither Charny nor King John was a great champion of knightly sport. John's letter of election makes it clear that no one will gain a seat at the Table of Honor by excelling at the tournament or the joust — those places were reserved for those who excelled at warlike deeds, *armes de guerre*. Charny began his *Book of Chivalry* by classifying the common deeds of arms along a simple ascending scale according to the skills needed and the dangers encountered: jousting is the lowest on the scale, tourneying second, and war the most challenging.[19] Both the initial classification and what follows show that war is the essential pursuit of the knight or man-at-arms — it is easy enough to guess Charny's own answer to war question 91. In the *Questions,* Charny establishes the same hierarchy of values. Twenty questions are devoted to the joust, twenty-one to the tourney, and the final ninety-three to war; thus, more than two-thirds are about the most serious pursuit.

Yet if Charny believed that the man-at-arms must be essentially a man of war, he is one of a very few writers who made a close connection between the law of arms and friendly competition between warriors.[20] Why was he interested? Although Charny thought such sports were no more than a preparation for war, he recognized nevertheless that they were an integral part of the pursuit of arms. If war generated the most important issues and the most vexing legal problems, the joust and tournament, as martial pursuits, were also regulated within the legal framework that governed the life of arms. Charny refers to the law of arms in both the jousting and tournament questions, and uses the phrase "the law of arms for jousting" once and "the law of arms for tournaments" several times. These subcategories of the law of arms were in his view a necessary part of a knight's education.

I have followed my own inclinations and interests in writing on Charny's questions on jousts and tournaments. The *Questions* as a whole deserve a full investigation, based on the modern scholarship concerning the law of arms for war. I, however, am attracted to the unique material on chivalric sport. It is a difficult subject and any reader will soon see how much is left in doubt by the closest examination. There is not much relevant comparative material to help with the many uncertainties that emerge from Charny's work. Texts concerned with the organization of tournaments and jousts are scarce, as are those concerned with the details of combat and its regulation.

In the course of this investigation I have found several documents of some use in interpreting Charny. Some are regulatory in nature, such as the English *Statuta Armorum* of 1292,[21] or the Italian, English and German jousting rules composed in the 1460s and 70s.[22] One, Jacques Bretel's *Le Tournoi de Chauvency,* is a detailed verse description of a touament of 1285.[23] Two fifteenth-century treatises on the organization of tournaments, René of Anjou's *Traictié de la forme et devis d'ung tournoy*[24] (composed about 1450) and *La maniére et ordonnance ancienne du tournoy* of Jean Courtois, Sicily Herald of Alfonso V of Aragon (written before 1437),[25] touch on points that also interested Charny. Closer to Charny's time, two formal announcements for jousts of the 1390s survive, while Froissart, the late-fourteenth-century chronicler of chivalry, provides us with some detailed if not entirely reliable accounts of high-profile jousts. The fifteenth-century biography of the Castilian Count of Buelna by Diaz de Gamez also tells us a little about how French jousting was seen in a later period.[26]

Each of these texts sheds light on some obscure points in Charny's *Questions*, but there are difficulties in using them to explain what Charny meant.[27] First, none of them are contemporary with the *Questions*; several were written a full century later. Thus, we cannot be sure, even if René d'Anjou and Sicily Herald claim that their treatises were based on old custom, that the tourneys they describe would have been recognizable to Charny. Second, none of the texts address quite the same issues as Charny. Later German tournaments, for instance, were a method to establish who was and was not noble in a given community; thus the rules governing them emphasize matters scarcely touched on by the *Questions*.[28]

All too often, then, the ambiguities of Charny's questions can be dealt with only by applying logic and common sense to them; and the problem with common sense is that it tells different people different things. I have put Charny's *Questions* in front of many people — scholars, modern jousters, re-enactors, and personal friends — and found their ingenuity sufficient to provide plausible but conflicting answers to any of the questions.

Nevertheless, I offer the following exploration in the hopes that a careful examination of the text will prove superior to none at all, even if much remains uncertain. At the very least, this book should make the Middle French text and an English translation of the questions on jousting and tournaments widely available. Beyond that, I hope it will also add to our knowledge of chivalric sport in three ways. First, the *Questions* were an attempt, at least, to define practice in a specific context, that is, mid-fourteenth-century France. A systematic investigation should give us a better picture of how these competitions were conducted at one particular point in time. Second, if the answers to the questions are missing and sometimes impossible to reconstruct, the abiding concerns of participants in these activities come across loud and clear. Others have made the most obvious points, but I hope more can be said. Third, I think the *Questions* evoke the quarrelsome, ingenious, anxious knights of Charny's day, and readers should come away from this book with a greater appreciation of the culture of knights at this particular moment in European history.

Notes

[1] Preface to the *Questions;* see part II, below.

[2] For a detailed discussion of this order, see D'Arcy Jonathon Dacre Boulton, *The Knights of the Crown: The monarchical orders of knighthood in later medieval Europe, 1325-1520* (Woodbridge: Boydell Press, 1987), pp. 167-210.

[3] *Livre Charny* was edited by Michael Anthony Taylor in his unpublished dissertation (see Abbreviations above for full citation and note 8); I have cited the *Livre Charny* from the somewhat more accessible article of Arthur Piaget, "Le Livre Messire Geoffroi de Charny," *Romania* 26(1897): 394-411, which includes an edition of much but not all of the text.

[4] Richard W. Kaeuper and Elspeth Kennedy, *The Book of Chivalry of Geoffroi de Charny: Text, context and translation* (Philadelphia: University of Pennsylvania Press, 1996).

[5] Kaeuper and Kennedy, pp. 18-22; Maurice Keen, *Chivalry* (New Haven and London: Yale U.P., 1984), pp. 12-5.

[6] Kaeuper and Kennedy, pp. 3-13; for Charny at Morlaix, Kelly DeVries, *Infantry Warfare in the Early Fourteenth Century: Discipline, tactics and technology* (Woodbridge: Boydell Press, 1996), pp.140-4; Froissart's account of the attempted taking of Calais, Froissart, 5: 229-46, Johnes, 1: 192-5.

[7] Kaeuper and Kennedy, pp. 13-18. Charny was, in fact, named keeper of the Oriflamme in 1347, before the attempt on Calais, then confirmed as keeper in 1355; p.15.

[8] The *Questions* have been edited in two unpublished and therefore largely inaccessible doctoral dissertations: that of Michael Anthony Taylor (see Abbreviations); and Geoffrey de Charny, "Les Demandes pour la joute, le tournoi, et la guerre de Geoffroy de Charny (XIVème siècle)," ed. Jean Rossbach, Université libre de Bruxelles, 1961-2. Neither editor attempted a systematic discussion of the many unresolved problems raised by the text. Recent scholarship on the *Questions* seems to be restricted to the brief summaries of the issues raised in them in Barber and Barker, p. 191; Philippe Contamine, "Les tournois en France à la fin du moyen âge," in Fleckenstein, pp. 430-1; and Keen, *Chivalry*, p. 170.

[9] Michael Anthony Taylor, p. 137.

[10] Boulton, pp. 170-1 (estimated size of French *chevalerie*), 179, 190-1 (number of members), 210 (royal goals).

[11] In Jean le Bel, *Le Chronique de Jean le Bel*, ed. Jules Viard and Eugène Déprez, 2 vols. (Paris: Librairie Renouard, 1904), 2: 205; trans. from Boulton, p. 180.

[12] Boulton, pp. 180-1, 200.

[13] Maurice Keen, *The Laws of War in the Late Middle Ages* (London: Routledge and Kegan Paul, 1965).

[14] Maurice Keen, "The Jurisdiction and Origins of the Constable's Court,*"* in *Nobles, Knights and Men-at-Arms in the Middle Ages* (London and Rio Grande: Hambledon Press, 1996), pp. 135-148, esp. 146-8; Keen, *The Laws of War*, p. 258 refers to the cases published by P.C. Timbal in *La Guerre de Cent Ans vue à travers les Régistres du Parlement*, 1337-1369 (Paris: C.N.R.S., 1961). Keen comments on some of those cases in the text of *Laws of War*.

[15] *The Tree of Battles of Honoré Bonet*, trans. G.W. Coopland (Liverpool: Liverpool U.P.,

1949); Christine de Pizan, *The Book of Deeds of Arms and of Chivalry*, trans. Sumner Willard, ed. Charity Cannon Willard (University Park, Pa.: Pennsylvania State U.P., 1999). Bonet's correct surname is now generally thought to have been "Bouvet."

[16] Bouvet himself assigned the duty of administering justice to "the constable" or "the duke of the army" (*Tree of Battles*, p. 132). Keen refers to an untitled heraldic treatise of the fifteenth century in which it is said that a student of the law of arms should know *The Tree of Battles* and have "clerk's learning," but "should also follow the wars, for there [he] will hear of the judgments that are delivered from time to time, which are not mentioned in the *Tree of Battles*." *Laws of War*, p. 21 and n. 1.

[17] Keen, *Laws of War*, p. 35.

[18] Boulton, p. 173. The *Reglement pour les gens de guerre* was issued on April 30, 1351; the proclamation of the Order of the Star was in November. The text of the *Reglement* is translated in C.T. Allmand, ed., *Society at War: The experience of England and France during the Hundred Years War* (New York: Barnes and Noble, 1973), pp. 45-8. For discussion of its contents see Contamine, *Guerre, état et société à la fin du moyen âge: Études sur les armées des rois de France 1337-1494* (Paris: Mouton and EPHS, 1972), pp. 20-1.

[19] Boulton, pp. 200-1 on letter of election; Kaeuper and Kennedy, pp. 84-93 for Charny's "scale of prowess."

[20] The only other known to me is the fifteenth-century treatise by Sicily Herald, discussed in chapter 4 below, which states that disputes about conduct in the tournament are to be settled by "the law of arms" the day after, "by the ordinance and judgement of the knights." Those same knights are stated to have jurisdiction over other disputes, for example, over lodging (*hostelz prins*), which implies a general jurisdiction over the site of the tournament. See Ferdinand Roland, ed., *Parties inédites de l'oeuvre de Sicilie héraut d'Alphonse V roi d'Aragon, maréchal d'armes du pays de Hainaut, auteur de Blason des couleurs*, Publications de la Société des Bibliophiles des Belges séant à Mons, v. 22 (Mons, 1867), pp. 182-3. Such matters did not interest Charny. Both Bouvet (*Tree of Battles*, pp. 193-4, 195-203, 204-5, 206-8) and Christine de Pizan (pp. 197-215) discussed trials by battle in their treatises, but neither included any material on what Charny in his *Book of Chivalry* called "deeds of arms of peace."

[21] The text of the *Statuta* can be found in *Rotuli Parliamentorum* (London, 1832) 1: 85. For the best discussion of the text and problems associated with it; see Barker, pp. 57-60, 191-2. The earlier tournament decree of Richard I (1192), which of little relevance to Charny, is discussed on pp. 53-6.

[22] Joachim K. Rühl, "German Tournament Regulations of the 15th Century, *Journal of Sport History* 17 (1990): 163-82, and "Regulations for the Joust in Fifteenth-Century Europe: Francesco Sforza Visconti (1465) and John Tiptoft (1466)," *International Journal of the History of Sport*, 18(2001): 193-208.

[23] I have used the text and discussion in Jaques Bretex ou Bretiaus, *Le Tournoi de Chauvency*, ed. Gaëtan Hecq, 2 vols., Publications de la Société des Bibliophiles des Belges séant à Mons, no. 31 (Mons, 1898-1901). The more recent edtion of Debouville (Paris, 1932) was unavailable to me. The tournament is discussed in Juliet Vale, *Edward III and Chivalry: Chivalric society and its context 1270-1350* (Woodbridge: Boydell, 1982), pp. 4-12.

[24] Edited in Francis Henry Cripps-Day, *The History of the Tournament in England and*

France (London: Bernard Quaritch, 1918), Appendix VIII.

[25] Edited in Roland, pp. 180-3. On Sicily Herald, see Rodney Dennys, *The Heraldic Imagination* (London: Barrie & Jenkins, 1975), p. 76.

[26] For the announcements and the accounts of individual jousts, see the more detailed discussion in chapter 1, below.

[27] I have chosen to pass over the fourteenth-century literature on judicial duels because Charny was not interested in them, and because, if duels were "deeds of arms," they were certainly not chivalric sport. I have also not taken into account the late medieval manuals of arms discussed by Sydney Anglo in "How to Win at Tournaments: The Technique of Chivalric Combat," *Antiquaries Journal* 68(1988): 248-64, and *The Martial Arts of Renaissance Europe* (New Haven: Yale U.P., 2000) and now beginning to be published and posted on the World Wide Web. Interesting as this material is, it is of limited relevance to Charny's *Questions,* and demands separate and lengthy consideration. Finally, I was not able to gain access to a copy of Sarrasin's poem, *Le Roman du Hem,* which celebrates a joust of 1278; it is also described by Vale, pp. 12-16. By her account it says less about the rules and organization of jousts than *Le Tournoi de Chauvency.*

[28] Rühl, "German Tournament Regulations," pp. 166-7; Barber and Barker, pp. 62-7.

Part 1

Exploring Chivalric Sport

Fig. 2: *Jousting scene from the Manesse Codex, fol. 18r.*

1 Jousting and Jousters

Today it is easy to confuse the joust and the tournament. In the Middle Ages, they were recognized as quite distinct activities.

Tournaments or tourneys seem to have originated in France in the late eleventh century. This was a time when armored cavalry was newly important in warfare, and tactics were being developed that required much practice. The tourney was one method of honing the skills necessary for effective group manoeuvers. The team or troop that worked together best won the game, or the battle. In early tournaments, as in the battles of the time, team members combined their efforts to capture knights and their mounts; the horses and the equipment were kept by the captors, and in the twelfth century, at least, the defeated knights were required to ransom themselves, much as in serious warfare.[1] Tournaments, therefore, can be best visualized as mock battles, which might involve striking opponents with weapons — Charny especially associated it with the use of the edge of the sword[2] — or even wrestling them to the ground. Many early tournaments seem to have included a role for infantry, perhaps chiefly to cover the retreat of outnumbered mounted knights. The term *mêlée*, which originally meant "a mixture," came to be applied to the fighting in a cavalry battle or tournament and to mean "a confused struggle."

Jousts, too, were often competitions between teams, as we will see in a moment, but they were quite different from mêlées. In a jousting match, an individual from one team charged another and tried to knock his opponent off his horse with a lance. The opponent, of course, was doing the same. Both, in the mid-fourteenth century, were bearing shields. It was a dangerous sport, but perhaps more artificial than tourneying, because of various limits on the violence.

It has been suggested that the joust originated in the judicial duel, where one man risked his body to prove his right over another in connection with some legal dispute.[3] More likely, jousts grew out of individual confrontations that took place between armies or tournament teams before the groups themselves came into contact. Symbolically heavy confrontations between two champions representing rival armies have been part of many a warrior culture, and are well documented in medieval western Europe from the eleventh to the fourteenth centuries.[4] Something very like jousting seems to have been an integral part of combat from the twelfth century; picked warriors, especially skilled in the lance, preceded their troops into battle, attacking champions from the other side. Such preliminary fights (*commençailles*, or in Charny's *Questions, encommensaille*) preceded the mêlées in the late twelfth-century French tournaments in which the famous William Marshal participated.[5] Jousts apart from tourneys were certainly a feature of chivalric life in the thirteenth century.[6] In Charny's time the joust was emerging as a favorite martial activity. Although professional soldiers still sometimes scorned jousting as a presumptuous and foolish waste of time,[7] it was becoming popular to seek out adventures or "deeds of arms" in a contested borderland (such as the Scottish march or the Anglo-French frontier near Calais) became a popular pastime. Such adventures usually involved jousting.[8] Jousts of peace were increasingly frequent. Thanks to the financial records of the cities of Flanders, we know something about many jousts that are otherwise unrecorded. Some were competitions between the leading citizens, who took up the sport in imitation of the nobility; other jousts were for nobles only. Jousts might celebrate such important occasions as a royal marriage or a diplomatic event such as Edward III's offering of homage to Philip VI.[9]

The jousts to which Charny devoted the first twenty of his *Questions* were to some extent friendly, even domestic combats. He was aware of the jousts between enemies that might take place in wartime, and devoted a question in his War section (W1) to one of the complications that might arise. Similarly, "jousts of war" (with sharp lances) in more friendly circumstances were also dealt with in the later section (W3-5). Charny's first section on jousts by implication concerned a much safer and more commonplace kind of jousting, using blunted lances, which activity Charny considered a suitable introduction to the life of arms for young men, but an introduction only. *The Book of Chivalry* describes jousting as "a good pursuit, attractive to the participants and fair to see," one that takes place during "festivities," but an activity that leads some to "neglect and abandon the other pursuits of arms,"[10] such as war which, as Charny later shows at great length, involves long arduous, journeys and other dangers and hardships, and which has a seriousness of purpose lacking in the joust.

The jousts discussed in J1-20 took place in a wider social context of "festivities." There were, of course, occasions when knights indulged in "pick-up" jousting without much in the way of preparation (J3), but normally, the joust was advertised in advance to attract those enthusiasts whom Charny refers to in *The Book of Chivalry*.[11] Charny leaves other possible preparations entirely obscure. We know from other descriptions of jousts and tournaments and even judicial duels that chivalric sport attracted large audiences, and that at least the richest of the sponsors, the kings of England and France as well as the most prominent Flemish cities, spent fortunes to prepare the places of combat, and to erect special viewing platforms for guests of rank, especially ladies. Less important spectators must have been numerous, and the crowds inevitably would have attracted hucksters and other entertainers, eager to cash in on the occasion.[12] Charny and his audience, however, were entirely indifferent to these aspects of jousting. The questions focus narrowly on the participants and potential disputes between them. Of the non-jousters present, we are told nothing at all. Concerning the physical environment, we are told only that jousters might stay at inns. Inns were, in fact, the natural centers of much activity at both jousts and tourneys, and fifteenth- and sixteenth-century sources tell us that *a l'hostel*, "back to the inn," was the traditional cry closing a joust.[13] We would be grateful if Charny provided such colorful details, but he had a more utilitarian purpose.

The content of a formal announcement of a joust was a practical matter important to Charny's discussion. Jousting question 1 begins with a description of just such an announcement:

> An emprise for jousting is announced for a certain place on a certain day to deliver all knights of three lances and not more, and nothing else is announced except the prize.

This summary would have been entirely clear to Charny's listeners, but needs explanation today. The word *emprise* literally means "enterprise, undertaking," but in Charny's questions and in other texts of the fourteenth and fifteenth century it has the connotation of "challenge." *Emprise* also referred to a specific set of commitments and rules.[14] Thus, the "emprise" in J1 is a joint commitment to perform a "deed of arms" which is publicly specified in a *criee* (or "formal announcement"). In other questions, there is reference to the "those of the emprise" (less literally, perhaps "those who have made an undertaking") (J8), and to "the knights of the emprise" (J14-16). These same knights are also called *dedanz*, "insiders," or "the home team," while those who come to take part are *dehors*, "outsiders," "from away," or "visitors." Thus "those who have set the emprise" were on home ground, had made a declaration that they would prove their skill in a certain way, were in fact the hosts, offering a prize to anyone good enough to take it. The "knights of the emprise" were a temporary brotherhood that had assumed certain responsibilities to carry out an "enterprise," in the hopes of winning renown for both their skill-at-arms and their generosity to challengers. Such brotherhoods can be compared to the more formalized tournament companies of fifteenth-century Germany.[15] There was a degree of formality in Charny's time, too, perhaps even a legal corporate identity. In one question a wounded "knight of the emprise" is replaced by a retainer or perhaps a captive knight,[16] who despite his good service is "not . . . part of the emprise."(J16)

The *criee* described in J1 is a bare-bones one. We can compare it to two surviving formal announcements to get a fuller idea of what might be included, at least in somewhat later, high-profile jousting contests. In the spring of 1390, three French royal chamberlains, with the permission of King Charles VI, offered to take on the world at St. Inglevert near Calais in a month-long series of jousts. Froissart gives us the text of their challenge:

> From the great desire we have to become acquainted with the nobles, gentlemen, knights, and squires bordering on the kingdom of France . . . we propose being at St. Ingelvert the twentieth day of May next ensuing, and to remain there for thirty days complete; and on each of these thirty days, excepting the Fridays, we will deliver from their vows all knights, squires, and gentlemen, from whatever countries they may come, with five courses with a sharp or blunt lance, according to their pleasure, or with both lances if more agreeable.
>
> On the outside of our tents will be hung our shields, blazoned with our arms; that is to say, with our targets of war and our shields of peace. Whoever may choose to joust with us has only to come, or send any one,

the preceding day, to touch with a rod either of these shields, according to his courage . . . Every one who may come, or send to touch our shields, must give in his name to the persons who shall be appointed to the care of them. And all such foreign knights and squires as shall be desirous of jousting with us, shall bring with them some noble friend, and we will do the same on our parts, who will order what may be proper to be done on either side.

We particularly entreat such noble knights or squires as may accept our challenge to believe that we do not make it through presumption, pride, or any ill will, but solely with a view of having their honorable company, and making acquaintance with them, which we desire from the bottom of our hearts. None of our targets shall be covered with steel or iron, any more than those who may joust with us; nor shall there be any fraud, deceit, or trick made use of, but what shall be deemed honorable by the judges of the tournament. . .

Underneath was signed, Reginald de Roye, Boucicaut, Saimpi.[17]

Later in that same year of 1390 a third challenge appeared, a *criee* issued by Richard II, no doubt envious of the spectacular success of the French festivities at St. Inglevert:

Hear ye, lords, knights, and squires. We make known to you a very great deed of arms and very noble joust that will be performed by a knight, who will carry a red shield, having on it a white hart with a crown around its neck with a hanging chain of gold, on a green bank. And the said knight will be accompanied by twenty knights all dressed in one color. And this will occur Sunday, the ninth day of October next to the new Abbey near the Tower of London. . .

And the following Monday the said twenty knights, in one livery as aforesaid, will be within the said field of Smithfield, armed and mounted within the lists, before the hour of High Prime, to deliver all manner of knights who wish to come and joust, each one of them of six lances, such as they will find within the tourney field, the which lances will be carried according to the standard. The standard will be in the same field, and by that standard all the lances will be measured so that they are the same length. And the said twenty knights will joust in high saddles. And all the lances will be fitted with appropriate coronels. And the shields of the said knights will be covered neither with iron nor steel.

At those jousts the noble ladies and damsels will give a horn garnished with gold to the knight who jousts best of those without; they will give a white greyhound with a collar of gold around its neck to the one who jousts best of those within. And the following Wednesday the same twenty knights aforesaid will come to the said field to deliver all knights and squires whatever with as many lances as it pleases them to joust with. And the noble ladies will give a circlet of gold to the one who jousts best of those without. And one within that jousts best will be given a golden belt. And the lady or damsel who dances best or leads the most joyful life those three days aforesaid, that is to say Sunday, Monday, and Tuesday, will be given a golden brooch by the knights. And the lady who dances and revels best after her, which is to say the second prize for those three days, will be given a ring of gold with a diamond.

And whoever jousts the said three days with a lance that is not according to the measure of the standard will neither carry away nor be given any manner of prize or degree. And whoever jousts with a lance without an appropriate coronel will lose their horse and their harness.

And the Wednesday following the said three days of the said jousts, sixteen squires carrying red shields, and on those shields a silver griffin, mounted, armed, and riding in high saddles with white sockets and shields as aforesaid, will hold the field and deliver all knights and squires who come of as many lances as seem good to them.

And there will be given in the same field to whoever jousts best of those without a noble courser, saddled and bridled. And whoever jousts best of those within will be given a fine chaplet well worked with silk.[18]

The common features and differences in the three announcements can be seen on the following chart:

Table 1: Content of Jousting Announcements

	Charny (J1)	St. Inglevert	London
Identity of "home team"	N/A	Named	Number, rank and livery given
Form of combat	"3 lances"(blunt?)	"5 lances, blunt or sharp"	"6 lances" (blunt); As many lances as desired (blunt)
Rank of "visitors" invited	Knights	Knights, squires or gentlemen	Knights; Knights or squires (in different parts of the contest)
How victory will be judged	Not specified	Not specified	Awarded by the ladies for the "best" on either side
Prizes for combatants	Yes (unspecified)	Not mentioned (gifts were in fact given by the home team)	Yes (specified)
Other prizes	No	No	Yes (for two ladies)
Restrictions on equipment	Not specified	Yes (shields)	Yes (shields, spear lengths)
Penalties	No	No	Yes (disqualification for prizes, loss of horse and harness)

The Charny *criee* outlined in J1 is less specific but comparable to the *criees* issued forty years later. Charny has set out this minimal *criee* so that his audience can be asked to supply the conventions that any jousting emprise must include even if these are not explicitly listed. After all, even the rather full discussion of events and prizes in the announcement of the London challenge hardly covers all eventualities; nor could it be expected to.

The procedure followed in the fourteenth-century joust is reasonably well known from a variety of sources. It differed from the often-illustrated jousts of a slightly later period. In the mid-fifteenth century and later, jousts proceeded one at a time, with the opponents separated by a list barrier for the greater safety of both men and horses. Yet this was not the case even a half-century and more after Charny wrote. The biographer of Don Pero Niño, a Castilian noble who visited the French court about 1405, described the "French fashion" of jousting this way:

> There is neither one that holds the lists, nor joust of one man against another by champions assigned; but each attacks whomsoever he will. All are assailants; ten, or twenty or thirty, or more, take their place on one side and as many on the other. As soon as one takes his lance, the other at once grasps his; and not only one goes out against him, but in their great ardor it happens that two or three come forward together against him who has stood forth, notwithstanding their courtesy; for they see how the matter is going, never against one man does more than one man come forward.

But despite this statement, jousters did get excited, and make mistakes, as the same writer shows:

> Such was the desire of the French to meet with [Don Pero Niño], that at one time two knights came forward at once against him, and struck him at the same moment.[19]

In Charny's time the same procedure seems to have been used, and similar mistakes were committed, or at least were conceivable (J14):

> A knight of the emprise strikes his horse with his spurs, and two of the visiting knights, each one aiming with his lance, come against him. And the home knight hits the first of the two with his lance and knocks him out of the saddle, and the second strikes the home knight. And with the same blow, the visiting knight knocks himself out of the saddle; and at the time of the blow the home knight did not have a lance. Should the home knight win the two horses from the visitors? What do you say?

The texts, taken together, evoke an exciting, crowded, dangerous scene.

The normal competition involved running a specified number of courses; in a course opponents would mutually charge, attempting to strike each other as hard as possible. Targets are not specified in Charny's *Questions*, although he does indicate that striking the opponent's horse was against the rules and resulted in penalties (see J7). In the later fourteenth century Froissart shows that blows were allowed only against the shield or helmet of the opponent.[20]

In such jousts, the two riders ran straight at each other, presenting good targets. A jouster did not divert or dodge his opponent's lance blow, but tried to absorb its shock while delivering a harder or more effective one. Froissart's account of St. Inglevert in his *Chronicles* show us dozens of successful courses, and in vast majority of cases, both jousters hit each other, usually on the same target (either head or shield).[21] To run out of bounds or out of the straight line (*forcorre*) and hit one's opponent while avoiding his thrust was strongly condemned.[22] These off-blows may have been considered too dangerous, since coming from an angle increased the chances of being hit on the body instead of the shield. In actuality, however, an angled thrust was probably safer, since it increased the chances that a lance would break off rather than deliver the full force of the thrust.[23] More likely it was the lack of mutuality that was blameworthy. Modern jousters forbid "folding one's shield," or deflecting a blow with a shield movement because they see the essence of the contest is to both give and take a hard blow. A similar attitude can be seen in a number of fourteenth-century accounts.[24]

Froissart shows us a case of "running out" at St. Inglevert, in a joust between "Here-Hance," a Bohemian knight in the English queen's household and an expert jouster, and Boucicaut, the French champion:

> . . .they thought to give full strokes; but it was not so, from the ill conduct of the Bohemian knight, for which he was greatly blamed. He had, out of the line of jousting, hit Sir Boucicaut on the helmet (*car de fourcours mal deuement fait il consieuvy sur le heaulme messire Bouchiault*), and continued his career: for this impropriety, of which the English saw him guilty, he had forfeited his arms and horse, should the French insist upon them. The French and English held a long conversation on this ill-placed stroke; but at last the French knights pardoned it, the better to please the English.[25]

This was the single example in Froissart's account of St. Inglevert where only one of a pair of jousters connected with the other, and because of the way it was done, it was worthy of a heavy penalty. Charny shows a case involving "running out" in J7, which shows how a determination to hit an opponent who was just out of reach could lead to a foul:

> An emprise is arranged for jousting of either knights or squires, with the announced rules as above. So it happens that one of the home team jousts in this way with one of the visitors, and because he might run out of bounds (*pour ce qu'il forcoroient*), the visitor throws his lance and the thrown lance strikes its butt end on the ground. And before the front end falls down it

pierces the other's horse and kills it. Should the visitor give recompense for the horse? What do you say?[26]

The best blow possible was one that unhorsed one's opponent; in some circumstances, as we shall see, this allowed the winner to claim the loser's horse. Unhorsing also ended the match between two men, even if some courses had not been run. Yet if unhorsing an opponent was the most desirable outcome, it may not have been all that common. At St. Inglevert, says Froissart, the best jousters of France and England seldom knocked each other off.[27] Other good blows were possible and appreciated by onlookers: if a jouster broke a spear on his opponent, or struck sparks off his opponent's helmet, or simply struck a blow that clearly shook up his rival, it was noted and commented upon. By the mid-fifteenth century, the kinds of good blows were being quantified and arranged in a clear hierarchy, so that the results of matches could be recorded and scored, and an unambiguous winner of the overall contest could be designated. John Tiptoft, Earl of Worcester, probably following Italian practice, created a series of Ordinances in 1466 that became standard for English jousts. According to these rules, the best jouster of the day was the one who knocked a man out of his saddle or knocked both him and his mount to the ground. Lacking such a man, the best would be one who performed the difficult feat of twice breaking a spear by striking his coronal (the blunt, crown-shaped tip of a "lance of peace") against someone else's coronal. Lacking that, a man who struck on the sight of the helm three times would rank highest. Last (and normally?), the champion would be whoever broke the most lances. The Tiptoft Ordinances also laid down a method of evaluating lance breakings; a break on the helmet, for instance, was worth two breaks on the body.[28] There is no evidence that such quantification was used anywhere before the mid-fifteenth century. Charny did not feel it necessary to discuss what a good blow was or how one type compared with another. The single question that discusses picking a champion of the day is entirely concerned with eligibility (J16):

> A knight of the emprise described above strikes his spurs and in his first course is wounded and disarms himself; and another puts on his harness and mounts his horse to joust in the place of him who was wounded with the agreement of the wounded man, even though he was not at all part of the emprise, but is only to aid those who had established the emprise. So he jousts so well that none of the home team in the judgment of all comes even close to him. Who should have the prize, he who jousted so well, or his master for whom he jousted, or whoever has jousted best among those holding the emprise after him? What do you say?

The concern here seems to be not "what makes one jouster the best?" but "how do you award a prize defined in a certain way when circumstances have changed?" In other words, how should a potential dispute between members of the same jousting team be settled? Note that this is a dispute about a prize the home team is awarding to its best member; certainly there must normally have been another prize for the visitors, as seen in the London criee above.

We might like to know who were the "all" who were responsible for "the judgment of all" evoked in J16 and what criteria they used. Other sources indicate that at jousts the assembled knights expressed themselves vigorously about the performance of jousters,[29] and that in some cases the opposing teams may have awarded the prizes to the best on the other side.[30] Perhaps this explains who "all" were in J16. But we also know that ranking fighters presided and judged jousts, and that ladies sometimes gave the prizes. But Charny refers to such matters not at all. It is odd that the men Charny trusted or encouraged to judge many other very technical questions were not being asked to debate the question, how do you identify the best jouster of the day?[31] Perhaps, unlike John Tiptoft, Charny was certain that any given jousting contest would yield a clear leader on each team, maybe the one who had unhorsed more opponents than anyone else. Another possibility is that choosing an overall winner involved, and was recognized as involving, such considerations as the rank of competitors or other intangibles. If judges or the "ladies and damsels" who chose the winner in the London joust of 1390 and many other contests were routinely influenced by such things, perhaps Charny felt there was no point debating the selection criteria.

If the *Questions* are unenlightening on the judging of the entire jousting contest, they devote a great deal of attention on two related questions: what precisely was at stake between two competitors when they ran their courses, and how were these individual matches to be judged? and what acts were worthy of condemnation and penalty? These questions can be treated together in the next chapter, because both of them relate to what might be called the currency of mid-fourteenth century jousting, horses.

Notes

[1] Barber and Barker, pp. 1-27; Barker, pp. 141-5.

[2] Kaeuper and Kennedy, pp. 88-9.

[3] Barker, p. 145.

[4] Matthew Strickland, "Provoking or Avoiding Battle? Challenge, duel, and single combat in warfare of the High Middle Ages," in *Armies, Chivalry and Warfare in Medieval Britain and France,* ed. Matthew Strickland (Stamford, Lincolnshire: Paul Watkins Publishing, 1998), pp. 335-43.

[5] Strickland, pp. 335-7.

[6] Barker, pp. 88-9.

[7] Jean le Bel, in his *Chronique,* 2: 195, shows the English commander Brandebourch dismissing a suggestion for a joust between his champions and some Bretons because "this kind of venture was over too soon, and in it one got more of a reputation for presumption and folly than for honor and worth" (*car c'est une aventure de fortune trop tost passée, si en acquiert on plus le nom d'oultrage et de folie que d'onneur et de pris*).

[8] Barker, pp. 152-4.

[9] Évelyne Van den Neste, *Tournois, joutes, pas d'armes dans les villes de Flandre a la fin du Moyen Age (1300-1486)* (Paris: École des Chartes, 1996) is a detailed study of the Flemish urban tradition of martial sport.

[10] Kaeuper and Kennedy, pp. 84-7.

[11] Van den Neste's chronology of Flemish deeds of arms (pp. 213-332) includes numerous records, from 1350 on, of traveling heralds and other messengers arriving in Flemish cities to announce jousts. In 1365, for instance, a herald of the Prince of Wales came to Valenciennes to proclaim a joust in Gascony and was given 25 s. by the *prevôt* (p. 237).

[12] One of the earliest references to tournaments, an ecclesiastical condemnation of 1130, described them as "markets or fairs," Barber and Barker, p. 17, see also pp. 206-8; and Werner Rösener, "Ritterliche Wirtschaftverhältnisse und Turnier im sozialen Wandel des Hochmittelalters," in Fleckenstein, pp. 332-5.

[13] Anglo, *The Great Tournament Roll of Westminster: A collotype reproduction of the manuscript* (Oxford: Clarendon Press, 1968), p. 98 and n. 1. René's fifteenth-century tournament book (see chapter 4) says the tournament should end with this announcement: "Let the banner bearers ride out, leave the lists, and return to your inns..." René, p. 21.

[14] Michael Anthony Taylor discusses the meaning of "emprise" on pp. 143-4, with reference to François Ménestrier, *De la chevalerie ancienne et moderne* (Paris, 1683) and J.J. Jusserand, *Le sports et jeux d'exercice dans l'ancienne France* (Paris, 1901), neither of which was available to me. Charny's questions on war indicate that men-at-arms undertaking a specific mission during war also used the word "emprise" to indicate the common enterprise. For one example see W42, Michael Anthony Taylor, p. 111.

[15] Rühl, "German Tournament Regulations of the 15th Century;" Werner Meyer, "Turniergesellchaften: Bemerkungen zur sozialgeschichtlichen Bedeutung der Turniere im Spätmittelalter," in Fleckenstein, pp. 500-12; Barber and Barker, pp. 62-3.

[16] The replacement is said to be acting for his *mestre* or "master," a term used to indicate either the lord of a knight or a squire (T19, 20) or the captor of an unransomed man-at-arms (see W62 in Michael Anthony Taylor, p. 123).

[17] Froissart, 14: 56-7; Johnes, 2: 415-6.

[18] Cripps-Day, Appendix V, pp. xli-xlii; trans. adapted from one by Will McLean.

[19] Gutierre Diaz de Gamez, The *Unconquered Knight: A chronicle of the deeds of Don Pero Niño, Count of Buelna,* trans. and selected by Joan Evans (London: Routledge, 1928), pp. 142-3. Diaz wrote in the 1430s or 40s (p. ix).

[20] See Froissart, 9: 281; Johnes, 1: 614, where the Earl of Buckingham and other English lords are enraged with their own champion when he strikes a Frenchman in the thigh.

[21] Froissart, 14: 105-51 is the most detailed account of fourteenth-century jousting, though the differences between it and other contemporary accounts mean it cannot be accepted as a literal record. On the other accounts, see Elisabeth Gaucher, "Les joutes de Saint-Inglevert: perception et écriture d'un événement historique pendant la guerre de Cent Ans," *Le Moyen Âge* 102(1996): 229-243.

[22] I have only found a few usages of *fourcours* or *forcorre,* and am unaware of a detailed contemporary or scholarly discussion of the precise meaning of the term. Scheler's glossary, included in the Kervyn de Lettenhove edition of Froissart, defines *fourcours* simply as *"attaque indue, contraire aux règle."* Froissart, 19: 224, in reference to the jousts at St. Inglevert, 14: 142.

[23] Anglo, *The Great Tournament Roll,* pp. 41-42 and p. 42, n. 1.

[24] My source for the rules and attitudes of modern jousters has been personal conversation and private correspondence with practitioners. For fourteenth-century disapproval of a lack of mutuality, see the joust between Reginald de Roye and John Holland at Entença, discussed in chapter 5 below.

[25] Froissart, 14: 142; Johnes, 2: 444.

[26] Thomas Johnes' translation of Froissart describes one incident where two jousters hit on their second try by "darting their spears" (1: 613). The original French (Froissart, 9: 276) says *"à la seconde jouste il se consievirent, mais che fut en widant,"* which seems more ambiguous. My thanks to Will McLean for drawing my attention to this passage.

[27] Froissart's account of St. Inglevert shows that of the 137 courses run, only 8 resulted in someone being unhorsed. This account cannot be accepted as a literal record, but it is consistent with other evidence; see Anglo's comments on the low level of success at the 1511 Westminster tournament, *The Great Tournament Roll,* p. 38, n. 4.

[28] Joachim K Rühl, "Regulations for the Joust in Fifteenth-Century Europe," pp. 200-5.

[29] See Froissart's account of the joust between John Holland and Reginald de Roye at Entença, discussed in chapter 5 below; also the account of the joust between Here-Hance and Boucicaut at St. Inglevert, above.

[30] For an example of a perhaps-fictionalized instance of this, see Androw of Wyntoun, *The Orygynale Cronykil of Scotland*, ed. David Laing, 3 vols. (Edinburgh: Edmonston and Douglas, 1872), 1: 445-6.

[31] In T18, two worthy-sounding ways of fighting in a tournament are contrasted, and it is taken for granted that the audience will be capable of arguing that one or another is best.

Fig. 3: *Tournament scene from the Manesse Codex, fol. 17r.*

2 Horses and Horsemen

By the end of the fourteenth century, "jousting" could be used to describe a formal foot combat.[1] Some of the deeds of arms so memorably described by Froissart and the fifteenth-century Burgundian chroniclers include such pedestrian competitions. Charny, however, was the true heir of an older tradition, and the chivalric sports he was familiar with and interested in discussing were entirely equestrian. Accordingly, Charny's curiosity, in his questions about both jousts and tourneys, was invested in who had the horses, what happened to the horse if the rider was unhorsed, and what should be done when horses were injured. (There is not a word about injuries to human beings.) The debates proposed by the questions are debates of *chevaliers*, horsemen.

In the Middle Ages, horses were themselves a powerful symbol of nobility. Jordanus Ruffus, the thirteenth-century author of *The Care of Horses* put it succinctly:

> No animal is more noble than the horse, since it is by horses that princes, magnates and knights are separated from lesser people, and because a lord

cannot fittingly be seen among private citizens except through the mediation of a horse.[2]

A horse was not only a luxurious form of transportation, but also an essential element in warfare as practiced by the aristocracy. Warhorses were specially bred, the *crème de la crème* of the equine world, and correspondingly difficult to obtain. Cavalry mounts for men-at-arms were stallions, which, if they proved their quality and survived the dangers of military life, were also valuable as breeding stock.

It is difficult to generalize about the monetary value of horses used in war, tournaments, and jousting, but we know enough to say they were very expensive indeed by most people's standards. The English records known as the *restauro equorum* accounts, part of a royal commitment to compensate men-at-arms for horses lost on campaign, give us the assessed value of thousands of horses used for war between 1282 and 1364.[3] Each man-at-arms entering service had one of his horses — presumably the best — evaluated by royal clerks so that he could claim compensation if it were lost. These assessments do not represent the prices of warhorses on the open market — if there was such a market — but represent a compromise between expert, interested parties, namely royal officials determined that the king should not be cheated, and horse owners, pressing for the highest assessment they could obtain. Evaluation under this system gives us a customary range of values, in which the lowest value assigned to a warhorse was £5 and the highest £100. The record of the Breton campaign of 1342-3 (in which Charny was involved on the French side) shows that the mean value of horses lost by lords and the men-at-arms who fought in their retinues was often more than £10 and occasionally over £20.[4] Similar French records, also associated with royal compensation policies, show, for the decade 1351-60 that bannerets' horses were valued at an average of 270 *livres tournois* (£54), knights' horses at 103 *l.t.* (£21) and squires' at 40 *l.t.* (£8).[5] There is no easy conversion between fourteenth-century and today's currencies, but even the lowest assessment, £5, for a very unimpressive mount represented a lot of money. A well-off English peasant family at the beginning of the century might earn just a little over £3 annually.[6] A landowner who enjoyed a yearly income of £40 — eight times the minimum assessment under *restauro equorum* — would have been liable, in England, to take up knighthood,[7] putting him in an elite class that included at the very most 1500 men.[8] In France, the equivalent of £40, 200 *livres tournois,* was also considered the minimum income for a knight.[9] Assessments of the more valuable horses could be far in excess of the minimum knightly income. Thus it makes perfect sense that jousters and, as we shall see, tourneyers as well, were very concerned about the losing and gaining of horses.

The very first of Charny's questions (J1) asks what happens in a basic emprise if, in a given course, "one knight bears another to the ground and out of the saddlebows with a stroke of the lance. Will he who knocks the other to the ground win the other's horse?" Repeatedly Charny asks the same question or something very similar (J2, 3), or more simply "Will he win the horse?" (J6, 13, 15), or a more specific query that comes to the same thing (J12, 14, 18, 20). Clearly the hope of winning horses and the fear of losing them are central.

There appears to be is a fairly simple principle behind the questions: the jouster who unhorses another should gain his horse. This is consistent with the practice of tournaments in earlier centuries, and with the practice in war of taking the loser's property. Note Charny's first question on war (W1):

> A lord has his whole army before a city and is beseiging it, and that lord has many captains, and from other countries than his own. A man-at-arms who belongs to one of those captains leaves the army and goes to demand a stroke of the lance from one of the men-at-arms of the city, who sallies forth to deliver him. And having met him in combat, the companion from the city bears the one from the army out of the saddlebows

with a stroke of the lance and takes the horse and leads it away into the city. And this was done in the morning. And that same day, when evening comes, another companion from the army, who belongs to a different captain than the first, goes to demand a stroke of the lance from those in the city. And the companion from the city who won the horse in the morning mounts the horse which he has won and goes out to deliver the companion from the army. So it happens that the companion of the army bears the one from the city to the earth and takes the horse and leads it away to the army. Then he who lost the horse in the morning comes and demands it back as his own; and the one who won it in the evening says no. Many good arguments are put forward about it on one side or the other. How will it be judged by the law of arms?

Whatever the answer to W1, once the claims were sorted out and judged by the law of arms, one thing is clear. Between morning and evening, the horse that once belonged to the first companion from the army was the undisputed possession of the venturesome companion from the city who had unhorsed him. If jousting is modeled on such confrontations of enemies, it seems apparent the answer to J1, and other questions that differ very little from J1, should be, "Certainly, he who unhorsed the other wins the horse."

But if things were truly that simple, why are there so many questions about situations that differ very little, at least to our eyes? If Geoffroi de Charny was not a tiresome pedant, jousters of his time were capable of making many distinctions. Jousting was not war, or at least not always war; there were limitations on the right of the strongest to seize the horse. What precisely those limitations were, was not perhaps always clear to everyone. As in W1, there might be many arguments — some good, some not so good — put forward on either side.

For instance, it was possible for jousters to argue about when someone was in fact unhorsed. The two obvious indicators cited were being "borne to the ground" and being "out of the saddlebows." The repetition of these criteria shows that they were important. Charny immediately (J2) brings up the case of the man who, thanks to a broken girth strap, is on the ground but not out of his saddle, "his saddle being between his legs and the whole thing off the horse." Then there is the apparently defeated jouster in J18, knocked out of the saddle, "except that with one of his hands he holds to the saddlebow." To clarify this scene — would it seem fantastic to his audience? — Charny repeats, "otherwise he was entirely out of the saddle; but no more of him remains on the saddle except his hand." These arguments seem a little strained, but the figure conjured up in J20 evokes a certain amount of sympathy:

> A knight knocks another to the ground with a blow of his lance, and his horse with him, and the horse is not able to get up if the knight does not get out of the saddle. So is he able to get out of the saddle without the permission of the one he jousted with? And if he dismounts without the permission of him whom he jousted with, and the horse gets up, is he who knocked it to the ground able to claim the horse by the law of arms for jousting?

Charny is capable of posing even more difficult questions in order to explore the definition of unhorsing. What if two knights knock each other out of their saddles simultaneously? Do they have to trade horses, or can each keep his own (J11)? In J14, as we've seen, two visiting knights charge one from the home team simultaneously. The home knight knocks down one of the others, and then receives the blow of the second so forthrightly that the attacker bounces off and comes out of his saddle. The problem Charny puts before his debaters is that the home knight had no spear when his second opponent hit the ground. That jouster was unhorsed; but can it be said that the home knight unhorsed him? And what about the horse?

"What about the horse?" is the issue that gives reality to these scenarios that seem rather strained today, and may well have seem strained then, too. (We must remember, though, that Pero Niño's biographer claimed that his hero had lived the scenario seen in J14!) Charny put forward these questions with a clear didactic purpose, with a law professor's desire to force students to think about basic principles. They were good questions because he and the other knights knew that if some of these unlikely scenarios did take place, there would be two flesh and blood jousters before them, arguing for their rights under the law of arms, with the decision having to be made by men like them.

Nor were these the only passionate arguments that might revolve around horses and jousting. We can identify three factors that differentiated one type of joust from another. First, it mattered whether the jousts took place within the conventions of an emprise publicly declared (*criee*) by an identifiable "home team." Jousting between the armies (as in W1) and simple "pick-up" jousting (J3) might be done without a *criee*; all other jousts were done in accordance with the declared rules (*criee*) and understood conventions of an emprise. Jousting done in the context of an emprise might be done with steel-tipped lances (*de fer de glaive;* W3-5) or with blunted lances[10] (by implication, all of the cases in the "jousting" section). Finally, whenever there was an emprise formally announced there might be a qualification by rank imposed on the competitors. Charny inquires about emprises of knights, or squires, or of knights or squires, either done with *fer de glaive* or with sporting lances. His questions are always about the loss or gain of horses. Is it normally the case that in an emprise for squires, for instance, an unhorsed man must give up his horse (J4)? What happens if someone enters the wrong competition, if a knight jousts in an emprise for squires (J13), or a squire rides in an emprise for knights (J12)?

There are hints that the obvious answer is the right one; that in jousting as in war, the horse would be at risk in any emprise (W5) and perhaps even in the informal setting of J3, where "knights are jousting without any formal announcement." But if it was always so simple, why are so many questions asked about the gaining and losing of horses?

There is evidence that not all jousts were the same. Class distinctions had some importance. Both Froissart's *Chronicles* and the records of various Flemish cities indicate that, in the early fourteenth century, some jousts were for knights alone, and others were restricted to squires. Indeed there were even, at least in Flanders, jousts in which the rich bourgeois competed with each other.[11] It seems logical that there were different rules and perhaps different stakes were appropriate to the various contests. Defining those differences, however, cannot be done with any certainty.

Charny's cases confirm that there was in fact a standing distinction between emprises for knights and those for squires. (He has no interest in jousting by non-nobles.) The *Questions* hint that the distinction between knights' and squires' jousts had something to do with equipment worn. Note the characterization of the knight in J13:

> A knight, *armed as a knight*, enters and jousts in an emprise for squires; and one squire in the emprise knocks him out of the saddle with a stroke of the lance. Will the squire win the horse? What do you say? What do others think?

Equipment is also important in the problem posed in J12:

> A squire, *completely armed for jousting*, enters an emprise for knights and jousts; and a knight of the emprise knocks him out of the saddle with the stroke of the lance. Will the knight win the horse, for each believed that he was a knight until he was down, but he did not wear any golden accouterments [symbols of knightly rank].

How would the Knights of the Star have considered the various issues raised here? Did actual rank matter?[12] In other words, was a squire to be castigated for sneaking in where he was not wanted? Was a knight "armed as a knight" disgracing himself or taking unfair advantage by playing with the squires? Or was the matter of equality of equipment more important than formal rank? (It was perhaps not simply a matter of armor — knights, traditionally better armed than squires, could also be assumed to have better mounts and more training.)

A little light may be shone on these controversies by other sources. We know that in the twelfth and thirteenth centuries there were martial games called *behourds*. The participants wore light armor or sometimes none, and their weapons were restricted, in many cases to lance and shield. Some early *behourds* are stated to be competitions between squires. Further, a fifteenth-century manuscript describes *behourds* as jousts between equal numbers rather than mêlées, one against one or a hundred against a hundred.[13] No one can be quite sure what the *behourd* was like, but the picture that emerges from scattered references is of a competition less serious than a tournament, a training exercise or a light-hearted if still somewhat dangerous recreation, one that could reasonably be done in lighter armor, and which perhaps was an early form of the joust.

What little we can see of Charny's "emprise of squires" gives a quite similar impression. The knight who takes part, apparently illegitimately, in the squires' emprise is armed "as a knight;" so is the squire who crashes the knights' emprise and remains undetected until he loses. The earlier distinction between full-blown tourney and more casual *behourd* seems to be replicated in the difference between the knights' emprise and the squires' emprise. If so, the knight might have been welcomed in the squires' emprise if he'd been appropriately equipped — knights did take part in *behourds* and *behourd*-like events.[14] It is harder to imagine that he was welcome in all his gear. Likewise, it is possible that a squire "armed as a knight" would be welcomed in the more serious, heavy-hitting knights' emprise. To take one step further into speculation, there may have been less at stake in the squire's emprise. The same fifteenth-century manuscript that identifies *behourds* with jousting between equal numbers also states that the prize for the best behourder actually went to the heralds who organized the event, since they received no fees for supervising a *behourd*.[15] Could it be, then, a squire's emprise was a low-cost, low-risk event in which unhorsed jousters kept their horses? And, contrariwise, that the squire in J12 likely lost his horse, despite his lack of golden spurs, because that was normal in a knights' emprise?

It is interesting to look at the *criees* for the St. Inglevert and London tournaments with these questions in mind. In the London announcement, there are three different competitions advertised: first, twenty knights will take on all knights; second, the same twenty knights will joust with both knights and squires; third, sixteen squires will meet both knights and squires. The first and featured attraction is restricted to knightly challengers, and no doubt ones of very high rank. The other two competitions are open insofar as rank goes, though of course those allowed to joust were certainly those whose skills would honor a royally sponsored festival. In the case of St. Inglevert, where the honor of kingdoms was at stake, the English visitors who faced the French chamberlains ranked from duke down to esquire, and there is no indication that there was any difference in the way they fought or were armed. These *criees* tend to support the idea that at the elite level, at the end of the fourteenth century, distinctions between squires and knights mattered less than skill. This is in line with the general social trend that, between the late thirteenth century and the middle of the fourteenth, elevated the squire from being a servant (if one with a specifically military, and therefore honorable, function) to being an independent gentleman. In connection with the famous Combat of the Thirty in Brittany, which took place at almost precisely the time that Charny wrote, the Breton participants were described as being *de toute Bretaigne la fleur de l'escurie*, "the flower of the Breton squirearchy,"[17] in other words, representatives of a respectable "order" of society.

Perhaps even in Charny's time, because of the "rise of the squire" and the existence of many experienced, well-mounted and skilled squires, the normal emprise was one for both knights and squires — one that I would argue played by the tougher rules associated with an emprise of "knights armed as knights." One can, however, almost hear the more conservative members of the Order of the Star, knights all, arguing for a more rank-conscious standard. If they ever did make that argument, the practice at St. Inglevert, a festival of chivalry enthusiastically supported by King Charles VI, seems to indicate that their opinion was obsolete by the end of the century. Where Charny may have stood in this controversy is suggested by a comment in his *Book of Chivalry*. In discussing the need for good men-at-arms to be motivated by a desire for salvation, he makes it clear that such men-at-arms need not be knights, "for many fine men-at-arms are as good as knights."[18]

These issues have taken us away from the question of horses; let us return to what Charny thought was essential. A final group of questions reveal another aspect of jousters' concerns with their mounts: those dealing with injuries to horses and compensation for them.

There are seven such questions. Two of them (J5, J7) concern a fairly straightforward principle: it is considered reasonable to require a jouster who "kills a horse with a stroke of a lance [to] pay for it." In J5 it is posited that such a rule is set forth in the emprise, and in the later question the same rule applies. In neither question is the compensation rule the matter of controversy; rather, the question is whether the jouster should be held responsible if (in J7) he was throwing the lance and not holding it when the horse was killed, or (in J5) a terrific collision between the horses follows the "stroke of the lance," and "both of them fall to the ground."

Injuries to horses might also be charged to those who were considered responsible. This may not have been quite as clear-cut a matter as the case where one jouster killed a horse with a lance-blow. Although a wronged jouster might look first to his opponent, he might also look elsewhere. Question J8 sets out this situation:

> A banneret sends out from his entourage some knights to go out with him in the fields to joust with those who have set the emprise; those knights agree with him and sally forth on their own horses, which are with them. If there are two or three of them whose horses are dead and injured in the joust from blows or falls, will the banneret be obliged to compensate them? What do you say?

Similarly, in J17, the replacement jouster "who . . . jousted so well" after replacing his wounded master is assumed to have struck a horse that day, "which horse is sent to him because he should recompense him." Charny asks, "Should he pay recompense, or his master?" The two questions reveal that an arrangement well-documented for tournaments was, in Charny's environment, part of jousting as well: lords attended competitions with retainers who fought with them. As we shall see later, fourteenth-century French and English lords were sometimes obligated by contract to provide their retainers with horses for both war and tournament, or to replace the lost horses of their men.[19] We do not have evidence that such an obligation was taken for granted, or necessarily applied to jousting. Perhaps the answer to these two questions was, "it depends on the agreement between master and retainer." Or perhaps, it depended on whether the knight who had lost a horse to injury had been unsuccessful in getting his opponent to pay him.

Questions J9, 10 and 19 indicate that it was normal for an aggrieved jouster to look for compensation directly at the man who had caused the injury. They concern what were seen as the reasonable limits to such a demand. Question J9 presents us with a joust of three courses. In the first course the knight of the home team "strikes the visitor's horse on the head or some other part." But the visitor doesn't want to quit, and rides the other two courses; only then "he sends the horse to the defender and demands that he compensate him."

In J10, a horse is struck by a lance, and the rider immediately dismounts and sends it to his inn. "The next day he sends it to the inn of the man who struck it," again with the expectation of compensation. Charny asks, "Will he pay him [for it]?" In both these cases it is fairly easy to reconstruct objections. In the case of J9, the knight from the home team would surely say that the visiting knight was trying to have it both ways: he wanted to use the horse for two courses in an effort to unseat the first knight and then, when unsuccessful, tried to gain the price of a horse by making a claim based on the blow struck earlier. If the horse was that badly hurt, shouldn't the visitor have made his claim immediately? In the case of J10, the knight being dunned might want to know why there was a delay in asking for compensation. He might even voice suspicions that the horse was not so badly injured when it left the field the day before, or that the horse presented was not the same horse at all!

We, of course, cannot be sure that these objections would win the day — further arguments for the claimants are easy to devise. If, however, Charny does not mislead us with these questions, the dynamics of such situations can be reconstructed. Under some circumstances, if one jouster inflicted an injury on his opponent's horse, the opponent could send the horse over with a request for payment: in a more modern phrase, "you broke it, you buy it." Moments like this were fraught with tension. The owner set a price on the injured horse, and it did not always seem a fair one to his opponent. The question may well have involved the pride of the claimant as well as his financial well-being. It has been argued, indeed, that the valuations given warhorses under *restauro equorum* were affected as much by perceptions of the owner's personal status as the actual condition of the horse.[20] We can expect that it was much the same in unresolved jousting disputes. The immediately relevant points would be complicated enough; there would be arguments made not just about the value of the horse, but about what actually happened, even, if J10 is in the least realistic, about the identity of the horse. Anyone who has ever bought a horse and been disappointed in the seller's presentation of the beast will not find these possibilities entirely far-fetched. The moment that others were appealed to for judgment, the matter would be further complicated by personal considerations, in other words, how each of the contenders was viewed by the community of jousters, and how much support he could muster for his claim.

The horse-trading aspect of a jousting contest is evoked very nicely in J19:

> A knight or a squire has borrowed a horse for jousting from another companion and he jousts on; but nevertheless he happens to crash the horse into his companion's horse and equipment. When after three weeks or a month this companion returns the horse to the one from whom he borrowed it, that horse has not gained [i.e. recovered] any value from the blows in any way that could be seen. And the companion who lent it refuses to take it, because of the blows, but wants to have the price of the horse.

There is a certain ambiguity here. Is the "companion" who lent the injured horse the same "companion" whom that horse crashed into? If so, then the question's piquancy comes from the fact that each man feels cheated by the other. The lender feels that he should get back the horse in the same condition as he lent it; the borrower feels that the lender is as responsible for the horse's current condition as anyone else, and in a normal jousting situation might be paying compensation. No wonder "they are in contention!" A detached observer might want to ask these men what their expectations were, and why their agreement, oral or written, didn't cover such an obvious contingency, but a more sympathetic eye can see the reason for upset.

Charny's jousters are revealed by his questions as men who are keenly aware of the price and condition of horses, and of the risks of losing their horses one way or another. Partly this is an artifact of the format of the *Questions*. Without disagreement and a bone of contention, there is no need for legal discussion at all. But the focus on the jouster's mount is a natural one. Horses of even middling quality have never been cheap; horses are easily injured or lamed; horses were essential to the sport and the participation of each competitor; horses, indeed, were a symbol of rank. Jousters, and Charny, might be content to let judges or hosts decide on the champion of the day without serious argument. They could not afford to be so easy-going about the rules governing their animals.

Notes

[1] M. Aug. Scheler, *Glossaire,* in Froissart, 19: 267. Also see Froissart, 9: 327 (account of the foot-combats at Vannes).

[2] R.H.C. Davis, "The Medieval Warhorse," in *Horses in European Economic History: A preliminary canter*, ed. F.M.L. Thompson (Reading: British Agricultural History Society, 1983), p. 19.

[3] Andrew Ayton, *Knights and Warhorses: Military service and the English aristocracy under Edward III*. Paperback ed. (Woodbridge: Boydell Press, 1999), p. 49-50.

[4] Ayton, pp. 69 (£5 pound minimum), 70 (standard values).

[5] Contamine, *Guerre, état, et société,* pp. 655-6; Jonathon Sumption, *The Hundred Years War,* vol. 2, *Trial by Fire* (Philadelphia: University of Pennsylvania Press, 1990), p. 218.

[6] Christopher Dyer, *Standards of Living in the Later Middle Ages: Social change in England c. 1200-1520* (Cambridge: Cambridge U.P., 1989), p. 115.

[7] For the history of "distraint of knighthood" (compulsory knighthood) in the fourteenth century, see Michael Powicke, *Military Obligation in Medieval England: A study in liberty and duty* (Oxford: Clarendon Press, 1962), pp. 170-8.

[8] Chris Given-Wilson, *The English Nobility in the Late Middle Ages: The fourteenth-century political community* (London and New York: Routledge, 1987) pp. 69-70; Peter Coss, *The Knight in Medieval England, 1000-1400* (Coshohocken, Pa.: Combined Books, 1993), pp. 82-4, 104.

[9] Sumption, *The Hundred Years War,* vol. 1, *Trial by Battle* (Philadelphia: University of Pennsylvania Press, 1990), p. 30.

[10] Blunted lances (those tipped with coronels) were usually called *rochets,* as in Froissart, 14: 56, but the word is not used by Charny in the *Questions.*

[11] Van den Neste discusses both noble and bourgeois jousts at length throughout her book, notably on pp. 140-3, where she tries to determine whether nobles and bourgeois jousted against each other. Froissart records an early fourteenth-century joust where it appears that separate competitions were held for knights and squires; at least separate prizes were awarded. Froissart, 3: 318-9.

[12] In the late fifteenth-century German tournament regulations, rank was exceedingly

important. Rühl, "German Tournament Regulations," pp. 166, 168-70, 176-7, 180.

[13] Barker, pp. 148 (squires), 149 (jousting between equal numbers, lance and shield only). Barber and Barker, pp. 30, 153 (behourd at Windsor in *cuir boulli*), 164 (a 13th c. German behourd would have been a tourney if they had worn armor); 165 (Italian behourds played with no armor, only lance and shield).

[14] Barker, pp. 148-9.

[15] Barker, p. 149.

[16] The rise of the squire followed similar but not identical courses in England in France. See Edouard Perroy, "Social Mobility among the French *Noblesse* in the Later Middle Ages," *Past and Present* 21 (1962): 25-38; Peter Coss, "Knights, Esquires and the Origins of Social Gradation in England," *Transactions of the Royal Historical Society*, 6th ser., 5 (1995): 155-78; Keen, "Heraldry and Hierarchy: Esquires and Gentlemen," in *Orders and Hierarchies in Late Medieval and Renaissance Europe,* ed. Jeffrey Denton (Toronto: University of Toronto Press, 1999), pp. 94-108.

[17] Henry Raymond Brush, "La Bataille de trente Anglois et de trente Bretons," *Modern Philology*, 10 (1912-3): 100.

[18] Kaeuper and Kennedy, pp. 176-7. Keen, *Chivalry,* p. 13, notes that Charny speaks of "men-at-arms" throughout the work.

[19] Barker, pp. 27-8, 120; Ayton, pp. 86-8.

[20] Ayton, pp. 60-1, 69.

Fig.4: *Tournament scene from the Manesse Codex, fol. 52r.*

3. The Jousting Scene— Some Incautious Speculation

In the previous two chapters I have presented a few speculative ideas when it seemed possible that they might illuminate difficult issues raised by the questions. In this chapter, I will go further, and make an incautious attempt to reconstruct the jousting scene as known to Charny and his contemporaries. I will be filling in some of the big blanks in the picture his questions present. My efforts are based on logic and analogy and not on an abundant documentation that simply does not exist. Readers may feel some of my guesses to go much too far past the evidence. I offer them, however, in the hopes that the guesswork may suggest the richness of the real-life activity behind the fragments of documentation. Jousting in the fourteenth century was a matter of exertion, sweat, blood, even, on occasion, violent death. Yet at the same time it was enjoyable and admirable, both to participants and spectators. Only some of the tensions and excitements surrounding the sport emerge in the *Questions*. This chapter is my acknowledgment that there was more to it than arguments over the rules.

In Chapter One some reference was made to major jousts of the 1390s documented by chroniclers of that time. Their accounts, especially those of Froissart, are the basis for our own scholarly and personal reconstructions of late fourteenth-century jousting. Yet do those accounts give a fair sample of all the jousting activity of their time, or of the fourteenth century as whole? Clearly not. The jousts discussed by the chroniclers are particularly dramatic ones. Most were confrontations between sworn enemies, made in time of truce. Even when blunted lances were made available to the competitors, they usually chose the more dangerous lances of war. Furthermore, all the larger jousts were rich contests sponsored, directly or indirectly, by royalty. They were the World Series or British Open or the World Cup of jousting, not the typical baseball, golf or soccer tournament.

We do not know a lot about the chronology of jousting, but it is clear that in a long evolution it went from being an obscure activity to one practiced only by kings. Jousts of individual against individual seem to have been part of activity at tournament meets (as *behourds* and *commençailles*) in the twelfth and thirteenth centuries.[1] In Charny's time jousting was recognized as an activity on its own and was displacing the tourney as the primary martial sport of noble warriors. At a much later point, jousting was only done in a royal setting — in fact jousting survived into the seventeenth century as a princely sport. When exactly jousting lost its popular appeal is uncertain. Van den Neste's work on civic-sponsored tournaments in jousts in Flanders suggests that the fourteenth century may have been its period of maximum popularity, for both participants and spectators.

Comparison of Charny's jousting questions, and particularly his comments on the activity in his *Book of Chivalry* with the elaborate accounts of end-of-the-century royal festivals of jousting suggests that the sport became considerably more important during the second half of the fourteenth century. Whatever his personal opinions of the usefulness of jousting, it seems unlikely that Charny could have been quite so condescending about it if, in his own time, major nobles commonly used jousting contests to build up their reputations — as they most assuredly did in the 1390s. The general silence of earlier literary sources about jousts *per se*, like Charny's own writings, argues that jousting had nothing like the status it had near the end of the century, when descriptions of jousting became relatively common.

I have suggested before that Charny's jousts were grittier and more domestic than the formal contests reported by Froissart. If the suggestion is accepted, it challenges us to visualize the contests of his era by comparing them not to St. Inglevert, but to more modest activities. I suggest that the dynamics of modern equestrian sports can be compared to those of Charny's jousts.

The modern horse show is not a single spectacular competition, but includes a variety of different competitions: not only there different activities, but certain "classes" are open only to riders of a certain age or experience, or to certain types of horses. Similarly, it is a poor racing meet that features only a single horse race. Reading over Charny's questions on the joust with eyes accustomed to this modern world of riding, it is easy to imagine it was common for the different "emprises" — of knights, of squires, of knights and squires — alluded to by Charny to take place at a single "festivity," either on different days (as at the royal London joust of 1390) or as now, on the same day.

To take this reconstruction a step farther, we can imagine that any but the smallest or most exclusive meeting of jousters would include a broad range of experience and skill — from the young novices taking part only in the beginner's classes (the emprises for squires?) to experienced knights who not only competed, but brought retinues of promising jousters with them. "Jockeying for position" may seem an excessive pun, but the phrase might well be apt. Modern riders and horse owners choose carefully what shows, which classes, or what races they will enter, because each event costs something and brings risk of loss as well as gain. In jousting competitions, the risks were much greater than they are now. Although Charny's jousters seem to have dismissed the possibility of personal injury as not worth dwelling on, they were obsessed by the possible loss of equine capital.

Modern equestrian sports are sometimes characterized as sports that uniquely involve two different athletes, of two different species. A modern rider, however hard he or she works on personal skill, is constantly thinking about his or her horse, its health, training and performance. At the same time, that rider is probably on the lookout for the next mount, a mount that he or she imagines — realistically or not — to be much better than the one currently being ridden. Concern about the current mount and the desire for a better are constants. Everyone knows that some of the horses on the circuit are far superior to others, and the riders who have those horses have a great advantage.

The search for the right horse has serious financial implications. The desire to be competitive pushes the modern rider to acquire the best possible horse affordable, or even one that he or she cannot really afford in the long run. Yet even such a horse is not good enough for the ambitious. Unless one has a large personal fortune to draw upon, the very best horses, those good enough to make the rider competitive internationally, cannot be obtained without the backing of outside investors. The modern rider hoping for Olympic gold in stadium jumping is dependent on the goodwill and interest of a consortium of wealthy fans or institutions desiring to be associated with a prestigious sport. Similarly, the best racehorses are often beyond the means of a single person. Ridership and ownership are separated more often than not. Even the very best Olympic riders must chase the horses and please those who control access to them, while in the racing world even the most talented jockeys are mere employees.

The jousting scene of the fourteenth century was different from the modern equestrian world in many respects, but some things were identical. There was still a huge difference between the average horse and the excellent one, with a corresponding difference in price. As today, acquiring even an adequate horse must have been a strain for many of the hopefuls who attended jousting competitions. Charny himself had no doubt that an inadequate horse would doom many a young jouster to failure. In the *Livre Charny*, he shows such a jouster struggling with a slow, unresponsive, weak-backed mount.[2] Beyond a certain point, progress must have been impossible without attaching oneself to the household of a great magnate or a king.[3]

There is no doubt that personal reputation — and the social and financial gains that went with it — must have been the primary driving force behind any jouster's desire to compete. Yet modern analogy suggests that the business of horseflesh was also a major consideration, even for the most noble. The consortia that own the best horses of the present day are no doubt motivated by a variety of factors. The intangible satisfaction of being involved with powerful and beautiful animals is certainly part of the picture; this attraction to horses, and their consequent prestige, continues long after they have ceased to be a practical part of daily life for almost everyone. But profit enters into it as well. Even the biggest prizes in the horse world may not be enough to justify the investments needed to support the championship horse; but the possibilities of profit through breeding are realistic enough to save investors from feeling entirely foolish about the massive financial commitment when talking with their accountants.

Great lords of the fourteenth century were perhaps less likely to feel foolish in front of their accountants, but they were not indifferent to wealth, which served as the underpinning of their position in society. We must visualize them, however, as being far more intent on the question of horseflesh than the most committed horse-lover among modern investors in horse breeding, and probably even more businesslike. The investors of today go home from a horse meet or a race in an expensive automobile or perhaps a private jet, either of which is a mark of prestige in itself. Those investors can continue to play an important role in society if all of their horse stock is liquidated tomorrow. The loss of standing in the horse world might constitute a considerable loss in personal terms, but that could be shrugged off without much consequence in the larger world. In contrast, the lord rode for business, pleasure or war every day, and supported not only personal steeds but also those of an entire household and extended retinue. It is difficult to imagine a great lord, or even a simple knight, who was not an expert on horses, or at the very least imagined himself to be such an expert. They must have watched jousts with eyes keen to improve their stock.

In the previous chapter I have sketched out the anxiety that must have surrounded the gaining and losing of horses at the joust, and the claims of compensation for equine injury. Beyond that I think we must imagine that the jousting meet served as the focus for buying and selling of horses, both by individual competitors and by lords interested not in single horses but in building up their stock for the needs of their entire establishment, and acquiring stallions for maintaining ongoing breeding programs. It is likely that jousts and tournaments, along with war camps and royal courts were the main venue for the sales of military-grade horses. The shape of even modern equine sports is due to some degree by the desire to show off horses to potential buyers: competitions in hunter-seat equitation display the qualities of a good hunting horse, while claiming races, where anyone can buy any competing horse for a set price, are mainstays of the racing world.[4] Perhaps more to the point, in Afghanistan, in October 2001, a buzkhashi organizer told a reporter that the traditional sport, reminiscent of the mêlée tournament, "helps us find and keep good horses, which are good for fighting."[5] A joust, and for that matter a tournament, brought the best steeds and potential buyers in a situation where the qualities of the stock could be appropriately judged.

Indeed we must wonder if there was any significant market, more like a later commercial market, for warhorses outside of these military gatherings. We have very little record of the horse market in the fourteenth century; what few records we have about horse production refer to the management of the royal stud farms, and royally-licensed importation of breeding stock.[6] The silence of the sources about buying and selling proves very little. Other considerations however, suggest a restricted role for non-aristocratic middlemen. As noted before, these horses were all stallions. An uncut stallion is a fierce animal, difficult to keep. In any era, most horse owners do not keep stallions, and even those who breed horses may prefer to use someone else's stallions for that purpose. Outside of the estates of the military aristocracy, there must have been hardly any stallions kept, and every trained stallion must have been owned by someone who could, and did, use it. It is difficult to imagine that even if one had the financial wherewithal, one could go to a convenient market and buy a horse for the joust, the tournament or war. The logical person to approach, if such a horse were needed, would be a patron of the higher aristocracy, and one suspects that such a patron would be interested in supplying horses primarily to his own followers. Buying or selling a warhorse would seldom be a purely economic transaction.

Charny's *Questions,* nearly unique in their approach to chivalric sport, give us a vivid if narrow picture of some few aspects of the joust of his time. Those aspects imply other activities that are wholly off-stage and can be reconstructed only by analogy to other equestrian activities of more recent times. If the *Questions,* in their unanswered form, allow us to restore only shadowy and ambiguous traces of a long-lost scene, the speculations presented here cannot offer clear support to any reconstruction. They are simply suggestions. They gain whatever value they have by being connected on concerns inherent in any sport involving horses. I hope, however, that this exercise may serve to alert my readers to the tensions and risks that may not be otherwise obvious in a modern society where few own or ride horses.

Notes

[1] Barker, p. 140-1.

[2] Piaget, p. 399, lines 41-53.

[3] Barker, pp. 117-23, for a discussion based mainly on tournaments and an earlier period. Froissart's account of St. Inglevert (14: 105-51) shows that many of the English jousters present were in the retinues of great lords who also took part in the martial activities.

[4] Perhaps the primary purpose of such races is to protect bettor interests by encouraging owners to enter horses at their proper level of competitiveness, but claiming races provide an important market for would-be owners.

[5] Geoffry York, "When It's Polo Day the War Can Wait," *[Toronto] Globe and Mail*, October 25, 2001, section A.

[6] Data on horse production and marketing are extremely difficult to find for the fourteenth century. The English evidence for warhorses is summarized in Davis, pp. 6-13.

The Tourney

The tournament or tourney was the classic "deed of arms of peace" in Charny's terminology, or chivalric sport in ours. The original tourney of the twelfth century was a confrontation between troops or squadrons of mounted warriors, very much like the serious battles of the time and using the same techniques. In the early fourteenth century, tourneys (as opposed to jousts and other deeds of arms) seem to have been reasonably frequent in France and England, but by the time Charny wrote, they had almost ceased to be organized.[1] Perhaps tourneys had become too expensive for potential hosts; perhaps changes in battlefield tactics made old mêlée skills less relevant; perhaps the joust, which emphasized a knight's individual prowess, had slowly been increasing in importance until the tourney proper became a nuisance rather than the climax of a martial gathering. Yet, if tourneys were, around 1350, nearly obsolete in France, this was probably not at all apparent to Charny: in 1342, across the Channel, King Edward III had held a huge tournament attracting a reported 250 knights.[2] Certainly the *Questions* treat the large, full-dress tourney as an important subject for a knight to understand.

Tournaments, mass combats between two large groups of mounted warriors, might be confused by the uninitiated with two other martial sports. Charny's Questions T15-17 challenge his audience to define precisely what constitutes a tourney, an *encommensaille,* and *toupineures.* The term *toupineures* (in other sources *tupinaires*) is an obscure one; it may derive from *topier,* an Old French word meaning "turn" or "tourney." No modern scholar, however, has been able to establish a precise meaning.[3]

Encommensaille or *commençaille* simply means "beginning," and it is easy to translate the word as "preliminary fight." It is a little more difficult to figure out how precisely these were run. When William Marshal was tourneying in the 1170s, *commençailles* were individual jousts or other small-scale combats between the assembled companies, which preceded the mass combat.[4] The thirteenth-century tournament at Chauvency was preceded by two days of jousts, which were not, however, called *commençailles* by the poet who described them.[5] Charny's T19 refers to *encommençailles* that took place at least a day before the main event, but does not describe them or allow us to ascertain whether these contests were jousts:

> A banneret is going to a tourney and has his bachelors with him in his retinue; and he wishes to tourney with it during the week. And some of the bachelors with him go out to the preliminary combats and lose their horses, without the permission of their master and without their master being there. When evening comes they request the return of their horses, and their master says no. How will it be judged by the law of arms for tourneys?

Question T14 postulates that if a tournament is taking place between two cities, and certain people are excluded from taking part, it may not be considered a tourney, but only *encommensaille.* This implies that *encommensaille* in Charny's time might look much like a tourney. We will look at this matter again when we examine the characteristics of a legitimate tournament.

Far more is said about the tourney proper, and Charny, if he does not give us a definition, certainly does provide information about how these combats were run. We are helped by the existence of two French discussions of tournaments from the fifteenth century. The better-known one is by René, duke of Anjou and titular king of Sicily, who in the 1450s or 60s wrote a plan for a model tourney, *A Treatise on the Form and Organization of a Tournament.* René's book is quite different from Charny's in that René was not opening up a debate but prescribing exactly what should be done to stage an elegant festival and deed of arms in what he may have seen as an antique style (though it must be said that in his heyday tourneys seem to have been making a comeback in both Flanders and Germany).[6] We have no record that René ever took part in one.[7] The second treatise, *The Old Manner and Regulation of the Tourney,* was written by Jean Courtois, known as Sicily Herald. Despite his title and professional association with King Alfonso V of Aragon, Sicily Herald was the product of a French environment, specifically the county of Hainaut in present-day Belgium. Sicily Herald died in 1437, and so his work is somewhat closer in time to the *Questions* than René's *Treatise*. Nevertheless, the gap is still large and we cannot tell what period of tournament practice, if any, Sicily Herald's description reflects. If we cannot too much on either treatise to explain the *Questions,* both are useful on occasion.

As in the case of jousting, Charny says little about the setting: little, but not nothing. It was normal in the later Middle Ages for large tourneys and jousts to take place in or near cities. Question T14 raises the possibility that a tourney might take place in an open area between cities, which seems to have been common practice back in the twelfth century; but it is clear that Charny thought that a tourney would normally be proclaimed in a city. As a result, participants would flock to that location. Question T21 shows us a knight arriving late, being unable to locate his squires in the crowds, and hiring in haste two others to serve him the next day.

René's *Treatise* includes the kind of proclamation that he believed would attract such a throng:

> Let all princes, lords, barons, knights and squires of the marches of the Île de France, Champagne, Flanders, Ponthieu first of seignories, Vermandois and Artois, Normandy, Aquitaine and Anjou, Brittany and Berry, and also Corbie, and all others of whatever marches that are in this kingdom and all other Christian kingdoms, who are not banished or enemies of the king our lord, may God save him, know that on such a day and such a month, in such a place in such a town, there will be a very great festival of arms and a very noble tourney with maces of one measure and rebated [blunted] swords, in appropriate armor, with crests, coats of arms and horses covered with the arms of the noble tourneyers, as is the ancient custom;
>
> Of which tourney the captains are the very noble and powerful princes and my very redoubted lords the Duke of Brittany appellant and the Duke of Bourbon defendant;
>
> And to make this better known, all princes, lords, barons, knights and squires of the above marches, and others from whatsoever nations they are, not banished or enemies of the king, our lord, who wish to tourney to acquire honor, may carry these little shields that will be given out presently, so that everyone may know who are the tourneyers. And anyone can have them who wants: the little shields are quartered with the arms of the four knights and squires who are judges of the tourney.
>
> And at the tourney there will be noble and rich prizes given by ladies and damsels.
>
> Moreover, I announce to all of you princes, lords, barons, knights and squires who intend to participate

in the tourney that you must come to the inns the fourth day before the day of the tourney, and display your arms at the windows, on pain of not being allowed to participate; and this I tell you on behalf of my lords the judges, so please excuse me.

Over a century separates René from Charny, but René remembered at least one practice from a much earlier time: Charny also expected the inns to be taken over by various retinues, whose members would display their arms together (T1). Rene's *Treatise,* as usual, gives detailed rules for armorial display:

> ...immediately after a lord or baron arrives at the inn, he should display his coat of arms in the window. He should have the heralds and pursuivants put up a long board attached to the wall in front of his lodgings, on which is painted his blazon, that is to say his crest and shield, and those of his company who will take part in the tourney, knights and squires alike. And he should have his banner displayed at a high window of the inn, hanging over the road; and for doing this the heralds and pursuivants ought to be paid four sous for putting up each coat of arms, and each banner, and they must supply the nails and ropes to nail and raise and lower the banners, pennons and coats of arms whenever it is necessary. And note that the captains of the tourney should do the same as the other lords and barons in front of their inns: there is no difference, except that at the windows of their inns they should display their pennons with their banners: and the barons who put up their banners at the windows are required on their honor to display the coats of arms of at least five other tourneyers with their banners, as a company.

Whether these rules or practices existed a century or so earlier we cannot tell, but the display of banners was very important to Charny; we hear about it in connection with a serious contract dispute between lord and retainer, during which the lord tries to force the other to "display his arms outside the windows with him" (T1).

René's proclamation finds no such echo in Charny in regard to other, quite important matters. René's ideal scenario makes the tournament a contest between two great dukes, who captain the opposing sides and act as patrons; Charny exhibits no interest in the patrons or hosts of his tourney, and there is no discussion of tournament captains, either. René's proclamation and other parts of the *Treatise* specify the weapons to be used and the livery to be worn by competitors. Again, Charny says nothing on these subjects. The proclamation promises an overall prize to be awarded by ladies and damsels. As in his jousting questions, Charny feels no need to discuss prizes.[10]

The proclamation and the *Questions* do find some common ground in regard to judges. René calls these figures *juges diseurs*,[11] while Charny names them *disceur* (T5, 6, 7). René specifies at great length who the judges must be, how they should be chosen, and what their duties would be. In his scheme, the judges — two knights and two squires chosen by the patrons and captains — are in charge of all practical and ceremonial aspects of the tourney. Charny, in contrast, shows his *disceur*, who are not identified in any other way, as directors of the combat.[12] Any other role they may have had was not relevant to the purpose of the *Questions*. Similarly, he never refers to heralds, who from an early date were involved in the organization of tournaments.[13]

What Charny says about the *disceur* allows us, however, to see how a tournament was set up. The first duty of the judges was to "take the oath of the knights in the accustomed manner" (T5). Charny does not specify what might have been covered by this oath, but René gives us a text in the *Treatise*:

> High and powerful princes, lords, barons, knights and squires, each and every one of you, please raise your right hand on high, towards the saints, and all together, as you will in the future, promise and swear

> by the faith and promise of your body, and on your honor, that you will strike none of your company at this tourney knowingly with the point of your sword, or below the belt, and that no one will attack or draw on anyone unless it is permitted, and also that if by chance someone's helm falls off, no one will touch him until he has put it back on, and you agree that if you knowingly do otherwise you will lose your arms and horses, and be banished from the tourney; also to observe the orders of the judges in everything and everywhere as they order delinquents to be punished without argument; and also you swear and promise this by the faith and promise of your body and on your honor.[14]

The provisions in this oath seem quite reasonable, and are paralleled in other sources, one at least as early as 1300.[15] Sicily Herald's treatise shows *diseurs* swearing competitors to use specific kinds of weapons and to refrain from interfering with any arrangements made by the *diseurs*.[16] It is interesting that not a single issue raised by these other oaths is treated in Charny's tourney questions. Charny does not ask, for instance, what should be done to a participant who strikes another with a sword point, or attacks one who has lost his helmet. Nevertheless, the oath was important to the conduct of the tourney. Questions T5 and T6 discuss what should happen if a knight will not swear: "should he remain to take part in the tourney or not. . .?" In T6, it is assumed for the sake of debate he has been excluded, and this seems the most likely answer. Without a commitment to fair play — however defined — no one could compete in the great game.

Questions T6 and T7 outline what happened next in a list of steps typical of the commencement of a tournament.

> the judge had "tie it up" cried and had the cords [*or* stakes] put in the fields, and people went out and the troops were made by the judges and they say "you are released" to them, and they assemble. (T6)

Since the question in both cases concerns whether a given contest is a real tournament or not, these actions seem to have had a legal significance. What precisely are those actions and why were they important?

The cry of "tie it up" (*le lacier* or *le laiser*) has been interpreted in a variety of ways, for instance as a call to "go out" (*issez hors*) or "go together" or "begin the tournament" (*laissez aller, lachez aller*).[17] Sicily Herald confirms that "*Laciés, laciés,*" referred to tourneyers dressing and armoring themselves, and indicates that there was a later cry of "go out" (*issiés hors*).[18] Lacing was the normal way of attaching both body armor and helmets, and as we have just seen, René considered a helmless man "out of the fight."[19] Charny's contemporaries took this reminder from the judges as an essential preliminary for a tourney.

Equally if not more important was the setting of boundaries to mark off the tourney ground from the surrounding countryside. Inside the boundaries the rules of a tourney applied; outside, combat had an entirely different significance. The existing text of the *Questions* is somewhat confusing about the precise nature of the boundaries. The first reference, in T6, is to *ataches*, which indicates cords or ribbons. In T7 and T8, however, these same markers are referred to as *estaches* and *estachetes*, posts or stakes, and this seems more likely both for textual and practical reasons.[20] Other texts indicate that the setting of stakes was a key part of arranging a tournament. Both Chaucer's *Knight's Tale*[21] and the treatise of Sicily Herald refer to a pair of stakes used as goals. Sicily Herald, indeed, specifies that there should be only two posts, "one for one side and the other for the other."[22] It is clear, as we shall see in a moment, that stakes were used as goals in Charny's time. The existence of other stakes cannot be excluded. Charny in T8 refers to someone riding "into the midst of the fields and outside all the stakes (*toutes estachetes*)."

It also fell to the judges to divide the competitors into two reasonably equal companies. This was a tricky job, since competitors came to the tourney either leading retinues, or as members of retinues, tied to a lord by formal agreement. Yet the need for creating two reasonably equal sides overrode the desire of individuals to fight beside their lords and brothers-in-arms. Tourney questions 6, 7, and 13 suggest that the judges created equal troops, in a process perhaps called "organizing (or dividing) the tourney" (*li disceur devisent le tournoy*, T7) by counting off troops or squadrons (*routes*), assigning them to one side or another. Something similar was done at Chauvency in the previous century: the home team, consisting of French and Lorrainer connections of the hosts, the count and countess of Chiny, and the visitors from Hainaut and farther north each chose a *diseur* to fairly divide the participants (*loiaument partiront le tornoiement*).[23]

After this, according to T6, the competitors were "released" (*leur dit quittié*). This might simply mean that the troops, once formed, were sent off to join one of the two competing companies. Sicily Herald suggests, however, that the "releasing" was a mutual act by the competitors on either side to excuse their opponents from oaths of fidelity and friendship that would normally prevent them from fighting.[24] Finally, according to Charny, the various troops assembled and — in some way that is not clearly indicated — the tournament began. Tournament question 13 says they "sallied forth" (*saillent hors*).

As in the case of the joust, the single important issue in the tournament seems to have been the possession of horses. In the days of William Marshal, warriors, their horses, and their harness (personal and equestrian) had all been at risk. No longer: Charny describes the action at a tourney as "losing and gaining horses" (T7).[25] When, in T9, some knights pull another to the ground, along with his mount, they "cut his girths and the breastplate of the saddle . . .lead [the horse] to the stake and the knight remains on the ground with his saddle between his legs." Charny associated the tourney with the use of the sword-edge, and in the *Questions* there are references to striking with weapons — in T8 someone is knocked off a horse, in T18 someone suffers numerous blows — yet the most natural word that comes to Charny's pen is *tirer*, "pull." In T6 "many [competitors] are pulled to the ground and their horses are taken;" in T10, two or three squires gang up on a knight "and pull him down and take the horse off to the stake;" finally, T18 contrasts a bold knight who loses two or three horses in a single day with another, more cautious one "who keeps his horse very close the whole day and endures and bears well the pulls and blows and everything that comes his way."

What legitimated the capture of a horse? Clearly, if the rider was removed and his horse led to the stake, the goal post belonging to the team of the captors, the horse was lost. In fact, the horse and rider might be taken to the stake together, and the rider then removed. That is what happened to an unarmed man in T8 (see below) and in T7 there is a reference to "troops...losing and gaining horses and [being] led to the stake." The fictional tournament in Chaucher's *Knight's Tale* alludes to a similar procedure of goal posts; in his story (and, it seems, in Sicily Herald's treatise) both knights and horses were at risk, and therefore the riders were not necessarily unhorsed. Chaucer shows outnumbered knights:

> ...being borne by force,
> Unyielded, to the stake by twenty horse.[26]

As we have seen in connection with T9, a question of legitimate capture might arise if a knight was not removed from the saddle (as we have seen in connection with J2 and J18). A perhaps easier question is found in T8, regarding who constitutes a legitimate target in a tourney:

A knight sallies out all armed without any concealment as above to tourney on a beautiful destrier. And when he comes to ride it to the assembly point this knight mounts a different horse. And an unarmed man mounts the horse he has got down from and during the tourney with the agreement of this knight continues on this horse into the midst of the fields outside all the stakes. So some others catch the horse and take it to their stake and knock down the unarmed man who was on it and they say that they have won it. The knight says no. How should it be according to the law of arms for tourneys?

One suspects this case was put forward by Charny simply to illustrate the difference between horse theft at a tournament and playing the game by the rules: although the owner of the beautiful destrier had brought his mount to the field, he had put it in the care of an unarmed man who could not reasonably mistaken for the original rider; the unarmed man took the horse outside the stakes which marked the tourney ground off from the surrounding fields; nevertheless some tourneyers, perhaps overcome by envy, took control of the horse, pulled it and its rider to their "home stake," knocked him down and claimed the horse. It would be interesting to hear how these hypothetical captors might justify themselves, but the point of the question seems to be that they had no right to capture mounts ridden by unarmed men outside certain boundaries.

Tourney question 10 provides us with a more puzzling case, which is concerned with defining not which horses might be captured, but who was allowed to capture them:

> A squire or two or three armed for the tourney find a knight outside of the mêlée. So they stop him and pull him down and take the horse off to the stake. When evening comes the knight demands his horse because there was no knight present at his loss. The squires say no. What should happen according to the law of arms for tourneys?

This question as posed cannot be confidently answered, but the background can be explained by reference to accounts of tournaments of the previous century, and rules and treatises of the next. Various earlier chronicle accounts show that large tourneys included not only men of knightly rank, but also their lesser followers. It was not uncommon for thirteenth-century tourneyers to bring along foot soldiers, even archers, who in certain circumstances intervened in the fight.[27] At various times, mounted men of lesser status were part of retinues, too: René's fifteenth-century manual visualizes each ranking participant being allowed a certain number of "mounted servants" (*varlez à cheval*) into the lists, "four servants (*varlez*) for a prince, three for a count, two for a knight, and one for a squire" as well as an unlimited number of "foot servants" (*varlez à pied*).[28] Similar provisions were in effect at fifteenth-century German tournaments.[29] Complaint about the behavior of such satellites led Edward I of England to legislate restrictions on servants in the *Statuta Armorum* in 1292. The *Statuta* prohibited all servants present on the tourney ground from possessing offensive weapons and wearing certain kinds of armor. Each tourneyer (*grans seigneur*), however, was allowed three armed squires who could take part in the action and pull other tourneyers from their horses.[30]

As we have seen before, the status of squires in both France and England changed considerably between the end of the thirteenth century and the middle of the fourteenth. They moved from being upper servants to lesser lords. The *Statuta Armorum* seems to catch them at a delicate point in that transition when they might be both servants and participants in the premier chivalric sport. Their ambiguous position in the *Statuta* allows us to understand the objection registered by the defeated knight of T10: he felt that the men who deprived him of his horses were not there as independent actors, but only as aides to a proper knightly participant. He visualized a tournament where the main action took place between knights and lords accompanied by their retinues, not one where he might face a mob of lesser men and the shame of being bested by them. What we cannot tell is whether Charny's audience, none of whom were esquires themselves, would have taken that objection seriously. Whatever the answer, the case presented in T10 brings home the potential confusion of the tourney ground, where the knights so carefully divided by the judges might constitute only a part of those present on the field.

Tourneys were meant to end at nightfall, but it was easier to start a fight than stop it, as T11 indicates:

> There is a tourney under mutually agreed rules and people are tourneying in it. When evening comes the stakes are taken up very late. But for a long time many knights remain on the field in a mêlée and they lose and win a number of horses on one side or the other. And when the evening comes many ask for the return of their horses because they lost them when the stakes were taken up. What will be judged in this case according to the law of arms for tourneys?

The principle here is clear: the setting of stakes is crucial in defining the game, and the drawing up of stakes ends it. Yet we might not envy anyone trying to enforce the rules in this case, or in the next one (T12):

> If it was said, concerning any of the horses above demanded that evening, that some should be returned, if any others delay until the next day, should it be decided that those horses should be returned, as if they had asked in the evening?

It takes only a little consideration to understand how tourneys sometimes got entirely out of hand and developed into hostile confrontations.[31]

Difficult as some of the preceding questions have been, another set put forward by Charny are nearly impenetrable. Tourney questions 6, 7, 13 and 14, taken as a group suggest that the results of a tournament might be challenged if every available knight did not participate. The first of these, T6, is a follow up to the question about the knight who refuses to take the oath:

> So the judge did not allow this knight to tourney, and this knight did not wish to arm himself, and the judge had "tie it up" cried and had the stakes put in the fields, and people went out and the troops were made by the judges and they say "you are released" to them, and they

assemble. And there many are pulled to the ground and their horses are taken. And when the evening comes, those whose horses are lost ask for them back and say it was not a tourney at all. How will it be judged by the law of arms for tourneys?

Taken in isolation, we might be hard put to make any sense of this. On what grounds are the losers objecting? The incomplete T7 sheds more light:

> The judges have "tie it up" cried and the stakes put in the fields. And when all the knights are in the field the judges organize the tourney and some troops. And those troops assemble before they should have ordered the whole tourney into troops. And before they are able to order the tourney into the final troops there appear many more knights on the field; so the judges are not able to arrange any more of them into these troops. The other troops that are assembled lose and gain horses and are led to the stakes.

The implied question here is, "if the losers ask for their horses back and say that this was not a tourney at all, how will it be judged by the law of arms for tourneys?" The challenge to the results of the tourney, to the legitimacy of capture, is based, as in the previous case, on the fact that some knights who came to the tournament ready to fight were not been permitted to take part. Two more cases, T13 and T14, extend the possible grounds for challenge. It appears that some might claim that in a proper tourney all knights in a given city and surrounding area might be expected to take part, perhaps even obligated to do so, even though they had shown no wish or readiness to compete:

> A tourney is arranged with mutually agreed rules in a city and the stakes are placed and "tie it up" is cried and they sally forth. And at the point where they are outside, one or two bachelors arrive in the city who are not able to have their horses or harness that day. And because of this they do not remain, nor do they join a

troop nor assemble. Will this be a tournament or not? What will you say in this case by the laws of arms for tourneys?

If they are between two cities and it happens just as it is described above, will these be tourneying or held to take part in preliminary fights (*encommensaille*)?

These four cases raise difficult issues. Could a tournament indeed be retrospectively canceled or delegitimized because it was not inclusive enough? If this was done, was the tourney reclassified as some other type of competition, in which horses were not at risk? As in the case of jousting, we are unable to define different competitions precisely, or determine in which sorts horses were at risk (if there was such a distinction). Charny imagined that knights who felt that the rules of the tournament had been violated by a lack of inclusiveness would try to argue for the return of their horses, but one can envision both theoretical and practical barriers to the satisfaction of those claims. Question T14 teases us with the possibility that the term *encommensaille* might be appropriated to designate a contest where captured horses had to be returned, and if so, then a failed tourney might be reclassified as such. But Charny himself appears to exclude that interpretation in T19, which we have already examined. The knights bachelor in that case lost their horses in *encommensaille* and are petitioning their lord to buy them back. If horses were normally at risk in *encommensaille*, it is difficult to see what practical difference it would make whether the contest in T14 is called *encommensaille* or tourney.

Tourney questions 6, 7, 13 and 14 show that inclusiveness was a recognized characteristic of a "real tournament." In all four questions, some dissatisfied tourneyers are seeking a considerable concrete benefit, the return of lost horses, and driving the argument of inclusiveness as far as it can go, if not farther. Yet they ought to have had a real foundation on which to build their complaints, even if their fellows might ultimately reject their position. Here, then, is a rather speculative reconstruction that takes inclusiveness seriously. When a tourney was proclaimed in a city, the focus of that event was a single grand deed of arms, the tourney proper. Preceding that tourney were a number of other martial sports, *encommensaille,* jousts, *behourds,* perhaps even the mysterious *toupineures.* What precisely the rules applying to these other contests were, and whether horses were at stake is perhaps less important than the fact that everyone knew that they were not the climax of the meeting, that some at least of the knights and great lords and retinues would not take part in the lesser contests, but would save themselves, their best horses, and their best efforts for the main event, when, ideally, everyone present would take part. Considerations of both status and practicality would be operating here. Men of established reputation might not want to risk it in any other forum than the best available, a "real tourney." Victory in a tourney depended on the disciplined use of well-trained retinues, and it was only in the main tourney that entire retinues were committed, and that customary friends and allies would all bring their weight to bear. The lord who found that he had spent his efforts and squandered his equine capital in a contest where expected participants had been excluded for no very clear reason might indeed be very angry.

Question T7 is the most realistic of the four. We can imagine the shock felt by defeated tourneyers when they discovered that among that mob at the edge of the field were friends of theirs, armed and laced up but not permitted to take part. The other three cases are more far-fetched, since the legitimacy of the tourney depends not on any error on the part of the organizing judges (or on their inability to control a mass of impatient mounted men), but on the exclusion of a mere one or two knights, who might not even be close enough to the tourney to take part (T14). The questions do make sense, however, if we remember Charny's purpose and method: principles are to be illuminated not only by "realistic" statements of problems but also by extreme ones.

The debate over whether a tourney is legitimate shows us both the potential confusion of the tourney field, and the anxieties that arose in a highly competitive environment. Another aspect of lordly competition is seen in the final subject of our investigation of tourneys, a group of questions concerning the creation and maintenance of retinues. We have put this subject last, but it actually comes first in Charny's presentation.[32] Here is T1:

> So a rich man retains a banneret, or a banneret a knight, for a certain fee and for the season, and thus they are agreed; and afterwards they come to the city where the tourney has been proclaimed and arms displayed in the windows. So when the rich man or the banneret above comes without his banner and whole retinue, and another rich man speaks to the banneret or knight above, suggesting he should be with him for a year; and the banneret, or the knight takes the offer. Then the rich man who has retained him for a year goes to remove the banneret who is with the other and make him display his arms outside the windows with him. So is he able to do that by the law of arms for tourneys? What do you say?

The fourteenth century was a period in both France and England when the terms of military service, to king or to other lords, were being increasingly regulated by detailed written contracts or indentures. We have a number of surviving contracts in which knights or sometimes warriors of lesser rank are retained by lords for both wars and tourneys. For instance, in 1332 the duke of Burgundy retained a knight named Jean de la Planche.[33] When Jean de la Planche served at a tourney, he was to receive the considerable sum of twenty *sous* (one *livre*) and a horse, the last a significant benefit. English contracts of roughly the same period sometimes were sometimes more generous. In 1307, the earl of Hereford retained Sir Bartholomew de Enefield[34] for peace, war and tourney, in return for a holding worth forty marks a year. Beyond this, Enefield was provided maintenance for himself and his retinue during active service. At war or tourney this included feed for eight horses, board for himself, seven servants and a chamberlain, and, best of all, suitable horses for the intended purpose. Such contracts show us how expensive preparing a retinue for tourney was, and how high a priority it could be for a great lord. The assembly of a band of tourneyers was simply one form of the most obvious manifestation of the power of a military aristocrat, namely, surrounding oneself with numerous well-trained, well-equipped warriors. That the same men were retained for war and tourney,[35] and were sometimes offered precisely the same maintenance and recompense for each, underlines the seriousness of tourney, even if Charny classified it as a "deed of arms of peace." Not only were many of the same skills necessary for war found in tourney; an identical infrastructure was necessary for the two activities.

Thus the priority Charny gives to the questions regarding contracts between lords and their knightly followers at tourney: the count or baron without knights in his retinue, or even without the backing of knights banneret leading their own cavalcade of knights, was as helpless as the jouster without a mount. And though would-be tourneyers might have been easier to find than good mounts, first-class tourneyers, especially bannerets with good followings, must have been fairly rare, and sometimes the subject of bidding wars. In T1, the first "rich man" has come to a city where a tourney has been proclaimed, but he has decided not to bring his whole retinue and he does not display his war or tourney banner. Could he be economizing? Another "rich man" immediately snaps up a banneret in the first lord's employ by offering him a longer contract, one for an entire year instead of merely a season. The question is whether this new contract supersedes the earlier and unexpired contract. The unwillingness of the first "rich man" to lose his valuable retainer is the basis of T2, in which he tries to secure the return of the banneret by offering him a life contract; the bidding war continues in T3 with someone offering the banneret a heritable estate. Who would criticize a knight for being interested in a new contract when it might provide a hereditary basis for his family's advancement?

As so often, it is not at all clear how to resolve any of these question about the bidding for the services of the banneret. We can see some of the competing interests at work in such cases. The most obvious is the interest of lords to maintain a reasonably stable retinue, even if it was not being mustered at every possible opportunity. Stability of service is the reason why any employer in any age enters into an employment contract. Set against this interest, of course, is that of other lords to add promising talent to their followings, if opportunity presented itself. Because of these competing interests we cannot be certain how those members of the Order of the Star who themselves were leaders—princes and bannerets—felt about the inviolability of contracts. We can imagine, however, that the bachelors of the Order might have argued for yet another interest—the interest of the up-and-comer from the lower ranks of the aristocracy who hoped through service at arms (war and tourney both) to advance in reputation, wealth and rank. Surely they argued that at some point in the bidding war the much sought-after warrior would owe it to himself, indeed to his lineage, to accept the richer offer.

The question of total compensation would not be only one concerning the banneret, knight, or even the squires who followed greater men into tourneys: they wanted the best opportunities to use their talents on the field. The dispute in T1-3 was initially triggered by the fact that a banneret (or knight) had ridden to a tourney with his own expensive retinue only to find his lord apparently unwilling to compete. The knight may have been faced with a direct loss, if the lord was not paying tourney expenses on this occasion; more frustrating, perhaps, was the loss of hoped-for gain. Thus his openness to new offers from other "rich men." The banneret may have felt that this loss of opportunity constituted breach of contract. This interpretation is supported by T20 and 21. In the first, "a banneret comes during the week to tourney and does not wish to take part at his rank, but to take part under another as a bachelor." Some "companions [knights] who are retained by him for a year" demand maintenance, but are refused; they then feel justified in seeking a contract with another lord. In T21 we have a rather picturesque presentation of a similar case one step farther down in tourneying society:

> A knight and two squires are contracted for the tourney and for the year. The knight hastily comes into the city where he wishes to tourney, doesn't find his squires, and retains two others on the eve of the tourney. And when the morning comes the two squires who are retained for a year come before the hour of "tie it up!" and present themselves to him ready to serve him. The master refuses them for the day, for this day he has retained two others. Then the two squires retained for a year go to seek their gain with other masters for a year, and say they are able to do it. The first master says no. What will be judged in this case by the law of arms for tourneys?

These questions of "employment law" according to the law of arms for tourneys confirm our overall impression that the Charny's tourneys were in no way lighthearted pastimes. On the contrary, they were events where amateurs had no place. Although they may have been less bloody and destructive than campaigns in war, they required a tremendous outlay of physical assets and commitment of organizational resources. Even if we exclude consideration of personal danger—as Charny consistently does—we are struck by how much was at risk. It may well have been one's standing in the "tourneying society,"[36] that was most in danger.

Notes

[1] In her chronology of 416 deeds of arms in Flanders between 1300 and 1500, which is based on extensive archival material, Évelyne van den Neste lists only 25 events called *tournois*. Between 1350 and 1399, there were only four *tournois,* and vastly more jousts. In Flanders there was something of a revival of the term *tournoi* in the 1420s and 1450s.

[2] This event at Dunstable is recorded by Adam Murimuth, *Continuatio Chronicarum*, in *Rerum Britannicarum Medii Aevi Scriptores (Rolls Series)*, 93: 123-4 and Geoffrey le Baker, *Chronicon Galfridi le Baker de Swynebroke*, ed. Edward Maunde Thompson (Oxford: Clarendon Press, 1889), p. 75. Adam Murimuth's version notes that it took so long to get this huge event started "that nightfall prevented the affair from proceeding, so that scarcely ten horses were lost or gained."

[3] Contamine, "Les tournois," pp. 431-2, n. 20, suggests the connection with *topier*. Barber and Barker, p. 40 record Philip IV's prohibition of *tupinaires*. Barker, p. 151 mentions this and English prohibitions in 1328, 1329, 1331. For fifteenth-century heraldic speculation that it was a game with a quintain where a pot or *toupin* replaced the shield, see Barker, p. 152.

[4] Barker, p. 141.

[5] Bretex ou Bretiaus, 1: xix-xxxviii, 14-93; Vale, p. 5.

[6] Van den Neste's chronology (pp. 311-3, 318, 320) lists six Flemish tournaments in the 1450s, the decade in which René wrote. René, p. 1, says he used Flemish precedents. René also admitted to following the practices of Germany and Brabant.

[7] Barber and Barker summarize René's active career as participant and patron in *pas d'armes*, pp. 114-7.

[8] René, pp. 5-6.

[9] René, p. 10.

[10] Sicily Herald discusses the giving of prizes in some detail in Roland, p. 182; see n. 24 below.

[11] Cripps-Day, Appendix VIII, p. lxix.

[12] At the tournament at Chauvency, two *diseur* were chosen to divide the participants into equal companies. Bretex ou Bretiaus, 1: xxxix, 97; Vale, pp. 7-8.

[13] Barber and Barker, p. 45. Sicily Herald refers to *diseurs*, kings of arms, and heralds in such a way that the distinction between them is unclear; see Roland, p. 182.

[14] René, p. 15.

[15] Barker, p. 144 and n. 33 cites the rules invented by King Alexander in the romance *Perceforest,* and another fifteenth-century parallel.

[16] Roland, p. 180. What precisely the oath meant is unclear: *"...prendoient la foi desditz chevalliers qu'ilz ne porteroient espées, armeurs, ne bastons affaittiés, n'efforceroient les harnois ou estaches assises par les diseurs, et tendroient à bon le dit des diseurs."* It may be that the competitors were swearing not to use "modified" equipment or gear fully "prepared" for war.

[17] Michael Anthony Taylor, p. 147 n. 72 for the possibilities.

[18] Roland, p. 181.

[19] Laced helmets are mentioned in Froissart, 12: 120-2; see discussion in chapter 5.

[20] It would be simpler and cheaper to set up a number of stakes than to surround an entire tournament field with cords. René, however, described an arrangement where ropes (*cordes*) separate the two teams, and are cut to begin the combat: Cripps-Day, Appendix VIII, pp. lxxxi, lxxxiv; René, pp. 17, 20. Ropes also separated late fifteenth-century German tourneyers, and the rope was cut to begin the tournament; Rühl, "German Tournament Regulations," p. 169. There is no hint of such an arrangement in the *Questions*.

[21] See below at n. 26.

[22] Roland, p. 180.

[23] Bretex ou Bretiaus, 1: xxxix, 97; Vale, pp. 16-12. See also Sicily Herald, Roland, p. 181, where the "*diseurs venoyent par-devant les battailles et faisoient passer ceulx qui estoient ordonnés de passer pour faire le tournoy à compte de chevallier, touttesfois auxditz seigneurs soubz qui ilz estoient;* and Juliet Barker and Maurice Keen, "The Medieval English Kings and the Tournament," in Fleckenstein, p. 221, n. 32.

[24] Sicily Herald says once the battalions were drawn up, "*les diseurs…faire quittier la foy l'ung al aultre.*" When this releasing was done the tourney was *par accord* (a term Charny uses, but does not define, in T9, 11, and 13); when the mutual release was not done, the tourney was *sans accord*. The difference between these two kinds of tourney seems to be that in the first, all the combatants, in the presence of *diseurs,* kings of arms, heralds and select knights, came to agreement about which individual combatant should win an overall prize. In the tourney *sans accord,* there was no joint decision. The last knight unhorsed on the defeated side won a helmet as best defender, while the heralds decided who on the other side should win a sword as best attacker (Roland, p. 182). This distinction between what may have been seen as a "friendlier" and "unfriendlier" competitions may have existed in Charny's time but we have no evidence what he meant by *tourne par acort*. For another passing allusion see the *Livre Charny*, Piaget, p. 401, line 168.

[25] Sicily Herald's treatise uses similar phraseology twice in Roland, p. 182. The tournament ends with kings of arms pulling up the stakes and telling the knights "*vous ne poez huy perdre ne gaignier cheval.*" The treatise says disputes over *chevaux gaigniés ou perdus* are to be settled the day after the tournament by *droit d'armes*.

[26] Geoffrey Chaucer, *The Canterbury Tales,* trans. Nevill Coghill, reprint ed. (London: Cresset Press, 1986), p. 53; Roland, pp. 180-1. It is not entirely clear from the treatise whether knights were ransomed in the tournaments visualized by Sicily Herald; at the very least it seems they were not allowed to leave captivity before the end of the competition. Question T18 (see just above) indicates that there was no such restriction in Charny's tourneys.

[27] Barker, pp. 24-5, 142.

[28] René, p. 15; Cripps-Day, Appendix VIII, p. lxxx.

[29] Rühl, "German Tournament Regulations," p. 171.

[30] Barker, pp. 57-9, 191-2.

[31] Sicily Herald, too, notes that tournaments did not always end when the officials wished; Roland, p. 182.

[32] The *Livre Charny* likewise implies the importance of a tourneyer attaching himself to a retinue: Piaget, p. 401, lines 153-6.

[33] Contamine, "Les tournois," pp. 428-9.

[34] Barker, p. 27.

[35] See Barker's extensive comments on the relation between war and tourney, pp. 17-44.

[36] The phrase is from Barker, who discusses the concept on pp. 112-136.

Fig. 5: *Jousting scene from the Manesse Codex, fol. 61v.*

5 Knights and Debaters

In *Chivalry and Violence in Medieval Europe,* Richard Kaeuper ably described the difficulties historians have always had in reconstructing the realities of chivalric culture from the surviving written evidence. Noting that "most chivalric texts press some ideal about chivalry to the forefront, " he regrets that

> no medieval writer went from one castle, tourney field, court, siege camp, battle line or raiding party to another, observing and interviewing knights of all particular social claims to record their commonplace attitudes and beliefs . . . lacking such a record, we have no oral history of chivalry, although that is precisely what we want.[1]

These words evoke the frustrations of anyone undertaking the necessarily endless and incomplete search for any lost culture that we can barely see through its formulaic literary reflections. For those investigating the lost culture of chivalry, Geoffroi de Charny's works have a particular appeal: his career, his purpose in writing, and his intended audience allow us to believe that his voice is one that the knights of his time must have recognized as one of their own. If his works are, strictly speaking, no more part of the "oral history of chivalry" than the writings of, say, Froissart or Ramon Lull, he was firmly rooted in knightly culture, and speaking to others also rooted in it.

Charny's *Book of Chivalry* hints at the eloquence of a knight rousing his companions to action. The *Questions* provide us with sketch of how knights related to each other, not when they were preparing or taking part in combat — the situation in which surely most of us visualize knights — but in giving counsel about how a professional warrior should conduct himself in matters concerning the use of arms, whether in war or peace. If the subject of each individual question is knights fighting, or dealing with the results of combat, the *Questions* as a whole show us knights talking, debating, and preparing to give judgment or at least expert advice.

It seems a narrow world. Perhaps the *Questions* exaggerate how narrow, since they are concerned only with subjects relevant to knightly expertise. If our examination of the *Questions* extended to the whole body of the text, including all 93 of the war questions, the reader would perhaps find it a little less narrow; the war questions include some philosophical conundrums that would make for interesting debates. Yet the entire work focuses on a few subjects — horses, prizes and ransoms, demands for loyal service or for compensation. Many elements of the warrior's life are not mentioned. One does not find such habitués of the battlefield and tournament lists as heralds, sappers, victualers, and servants (*varlez*). Only once do the ladies appear who allegedly served as the knights' inspiration and ornament (a subject Charny talked about at some length in the *Book of Chivalry*). Among the subjects that are almost never raised are the injury, maiming, and death of human beings. It is perhaps not surprising that the suffering that war inflicted on non-combatants is undiscussed — this is often omitted by writers who emphasize the glories of war. But the suffering of good men-at-arms is likewise passed over: the knights and squires, bannerets and great lords of Charny's *Questions* are practically invulnerable.[2]

The medieval man-at-arms faced dangers besides death and crippling wounds, however, dangers that were not too frightening to discuss, and these are the subjects of the many of the *Questions*. Among them were these: that a warrior might lose more in war, tournament, or joust than he thought he was risking, or should be expected to risk; that he might lose fruits of victory he felt he had legitimately gained; or that he might be excluded from participation in martial competition, and suffer not only a loss of opportunity but a loss of status. All of these risks might be moderated through rules and the enforcement of rules.

In the questions on war, Charny's problems generally address dangers that might arise if competition became too fierce, plunging into disorder a community of "companions" (a word Charny occasionally uses to mean "man-at-arms"), resulting in a savage conflict without bounds. To contain the savagery of war is the eternal goal of the "laws of arms." The laws of war are never fully successful in containing conflict, and there are always temptations to discard them as inconvenient or even dangerous, but the amount of effort over the centuries to devise, agree upon, and even enforce such laws shows how most war-makers at most times hope to set bounds on war, to avoid the frightening prospect of "total war." Charny's knights shared this common characteristic of warriors over the ages. Quite naturally, many of the rules *de guerre* which Charny thought they would be most interested in debating were concerned with knights capturing each other for ransom: ransom was the safety valve that reduced casualties among the nobler combatants. Charny's contemporaries were intensely concerned that the rules of ransom be clear so that the interests of both captor and captive were protected, profits were secured and bloodshed was avoided.

In the questions on the joust and the tournament that we have been examining, there is a similar desire to moderate controllable risks. The loss of a horse was not the worst thing that might happen to a jouster or a tourneyer, but was an extremely serious matter for a man who wished to take part in, and profit from, the honorable life of arms, and rules or custom could regulate the matter to satisfy most participants most of the time. These rules and others would make possible martial games in which even traditional enemies — in the later fourteenth century, the French and the English, or the Scots and the English — might take part without the bounds being burst, at least most of the time.

We have abundant documentation of the fact that tournaments and individual deeds of arms might generate as much tension as battle. Froissart, in his account of a deed of arms in 1387, shows this very well. During the course of a war between French and Castilian forces on one hand and English and Portuguese armies on the other, an ambitious French knight, Sir Reginald de Roye, challenged Sir John Holland, earl of Huntingdon, to a deed of arms including "three courses with the lance, three attacks with the sword, three with the battle-axe, and three with the dagger." Holland accepted, and a prestigious confrontation was arranged. Sir Reginald was given a passport so that he and thirty companions could come to the English war camp at Entença, where the two champions would fight in a limited but still dangerous way. In addition to the peril to the bodies of the two combatants, there was a risk to their renown, and to the reputations of their fellows, whom they represented. In the very first set of combats, it emerged that Reginald was using an unusual defensive tactic:

> Having braced their targets and examined each other through the visors of their helmets, they spurred on their horses, spear in hand. Though they allowed their horses to gallop as they pleased, they advanced on as straight a line as if it had been drawn with a cord, and hit each other on the visors, with such force that Sir Reginald's lance was shivered into four pieces, which flew to a greater height than they could have been thrown. All present allowed this to be gallantly done. Sir John Holland struck Sir Reginald likewise on the visor, but not with the same success, and I will tell you why; Sir Reginald had but slightly laced on his visor, so that it was held by one thong only, which broke at

the blow, and the helmet flew over his head, leaving Sir Reginald bare-headed. Each passed the other, and Sir John Holland bore his lance without halting. The spectators cried out that it was a handsome course.

In the second course, Reginald's helmet, again loosely tied on, again came off, while John Holland suffered a "very severe blow." Reginald de Roye's success in landing such hard blows was impressive, as was the way he frustrated Holland's strikes. But Holland's friends had now noticed how Reginald had fixed his armor and objected:

> "Ha," cried the English to the French, "he does not fight fair *(il prent avantaige)*; why is not his helmet as well buckled and laced on as Sir John Holland's? We say he is playing tricks: tell him to put himself on an equal footing with his adversary."

One can imagine the potential for a serious confrontation between two proud groups of warriors, still at war with each other, and angered (the French as much as the English) by slights upon their collective honor. John of Gaunt (duke of Lancaster and titular king of Castile) used his authority as host and ranking noble to defuse the tension of the moment:

> "Hold your tongues," said the duke, "and let them alone: in arms every one takes what advantage he can: if Sir John thinks there is any advantage in thus fastening on the helmet, he may do the same. But, for my part, were I in their situations, I would lace my helmet as tight as possible; and if one hundred were asked their opinions, there would be fourscore of my way of thinking."

John of Gaunt's intervention was effective: "The English, on this, were silent, and never again interfered;" In fact, "silent" is an exaggeration. Froissart himself shows that the debate did not end. Although the duke's ruling stood, the ladies present, the king of Portugal and his knights, the English men-at-arms, and John of Gaunt himself continued to discuss the matter and disagree about the legitimacy of avoiding the full force of an opponent's blow by the seemingly crazy tactic of loosely lacing one's own helmet.[3]

This account, like many of Froissart's stories, cannot be taken at face value;[4] but, like Charny's *Questions,* it suggests a real possibility of riot at even the most formal deed of arms. If that danger was most pressing when enemies, during truce or peacetime, tested each other, the danger of a serious falling out between erstwhile friends was real, too. How was this to be avoided? By the citing of precedents, among other things, as at Entença, when the Portuguese knight Sir John Fernando is shown telling his king, in support of Reginald de Roye, "they do joust well; and formerly I saw as good jousts before your brother, when we were at Elvas to oppose the king of Castile, between this Frenchman and Sir William Windsor; but I never heard that his helmet was tighter laced then than it is now." By the rulings of respected, experienced, and ranking knights, as when in the same episode John of Gaunt tells Sir Thomas Percy and Sir Thomas Moreaux (perhaps to still their further complaints?) that "Sir Reginald de Roye is not now to be taught how to joust: he is better skilled than Sir John Holland, though he has borne himself well." By talk! The internal order of the international knightly community, a dangerous bunch at the best of times, was maintained, in so far as it was maintained, by formal and informal discussion, by argument, by legal rulings and agreements by consensus, all of which were meant to distinguish the noble practice of arms from brawling, theft, and murder.

Charny's *Questions,* like the chronicle accounts of the fourteenth century and many other sources, show us that however much brutal violence the practice of chivalry entailed, or even allowed, chivalry was more than brutal violence. The safety, interests, status of its practitioners and promoters demanded that there be limits. And how were those limits enforced? Charny's *Questions* remind us that, in the considered opinion of this prominent, strenuous knight, discipline was as necessary as prowess and that this discipline must be based in part on discussion, debate, and judgment.[5] In all of Charny's writings we see a desire for the chivalry of his time to act as a order — a group governed by its own laws, acting to achieve part of the divine purpose. In the *Questions* the foundations of knightly order are revealed, and we see them as based on the concrete, unavoidable concerns of a self-appointed elite of horse warriors. Charny's philosophizing is rooted in practicalities. The *Questions* confirm Geoffroi de Charny's status as one of the Middle Ages' most interesting writers on the ideals and implementation of chivalry, and they themselves stand as a fascinating source that tells us much about the realities of the knightly life.

Notes

[1] Kaeuper, *Chivalry and Violence in Medieval Europe* (Oxford: Oxford U.P., 1999), p. 34. The importance of knights talking to each other, especially at tournaments, was also suggested to me by Mary Arlene Santina, *The Tournament in Literature: Literary representations of the medieval tournament in Old French works, 1150-1226* (New York: Peter Lang, 1999), pp. 49-50.

[2] Threats of death are reported in some of the war questions concerned with rights of ransom, and in W80, Michael Anthony Taylor, pp. 131-2 someone is actually killed, illegally, after being captured. Compare this reluctance to discuss death with the silence about fear detected by Andrew Taylor in "Chivalric Conversation and the Denial of Male Fear," in *Conflicted Identities and Multiple Masculinities: Men in the Medieval West,* ed. Jacqueline Murray (New York and London: Garland Publishing, 1999), pp. 169-88.

[3] Froissart, 12: 116-24, Johnes, 2: 228-31.

[4] The Portuguese chronicler Fernão Lopes records a quite different version of this confrontation; see Fernão Lopes, *The English in Portugal 1367-87: Extracts from the Chronicles of Dom Fernando and Dom João,* trans. by Derek W. Lomax and R.J. Oakley (Warminster: Aris and Phillips, 1988), pp. 276-9.

[5] For the role of "collective judgment" in medieval government, see Susan Reynolds, *Kingdoms and Communities in Western Europe, 900-1300* (Oxford: Clarendon Press, 1984).

Fig. 6: *Jousting scene from the Manesse Codex, fol. 192v.*

Part II

Charny's Questions on the Joust and the Tourney

Including Questions 1, 3, 4 and 5 on War

Demandes pour la joute, les tournois et la guerre.

[I. Jousting]

Ce sont les demandes pour la jouste que je, Gyefroy de Charni, fais a haut et puissant prince des Chevaliers de Nostre Dame de la Noble Maison a estre jugiees par vous et les chevaliers de nostre noble compaignie.

1. Premierement je demande:

Une emprise de jouste est criee a estre en tel lieu et en tel jour a delivrer tous chevaliers parmi trois lances et non plus, et n'a en la criee fors que le pris. Si avient que .j. chevalier porte .i. autre a terre de cop de lance fors des arçons. Celui qui le porte a terre, aura il gaaigné le cheval de l'autre? Qu'en dictes vous ne qu'en sera il jugie par droit d'armes?

2. Charny demande:

Si'l avenoit qu'en celle feste .j. chevalier portast un autre a terre de cop de lance, sa selle entre ses jambes et tout hors du cheval, celui qui le porte jus gaaignera il le cheval? Qu'en dictes vous ne qu'en sera il jugié par droit d'armes?

Questions concerning the joust, tournaments, and war.

[I. Jousting]

These are the questions concerning the joust which I, Geoffroy de Charny, pose to the high and mighty prince of the Knights of Our Lady of the Noble House to be judged by you and the knights of our noble company.

1. First I ask:

An emprise for jousting is announced for a certain place on a certain day to deliver all knights of three lances and not more, and nothing else is announced except the prize. So it happens that one knight bears another to the ground and out of the saddlebows with a stroke of the lance. Will he who knocks the other to the ground win the other's horse? What do you say in this case, will it not be judged by the law of arms?

2. Charny asks:

If it happened that in this celebration one knight knocked another to the ground with a stroke of the lance, his saddle being between his legs and the whole thing off the horse, will he who knocked the other down win the horse? What do you say in this case, will it not be judged by the laws of arms?

3. Charny demande:

Chevaliers joustent sanz criee, et porte un chevalier .i. autre jus de cop de lance hors des arçons. Gaaignera il le cheval celui qui le porte jus? Qu'en dictes vous?

4. Charny demande:

Une emprise d'escuiers se fait pour jouster par la mesme maniere que la criee dessus et non autrement. Uns escuiers porte .i. autre a terre hors de la selle; gaignera il le cheval? Qu'en dictes vous?

3. Charny asks:

Knights are jousting without any formal announcement, and one knight knocks another down and out of the saddle with a stroke of the lance. Will he who knocked the other down win the horse? What do you say?

4. Charny asks:

An emprise for squires is arranged with jousting in the same manner as in the announcement above, and in no other way. One squire knocks another to the ground and out of the saddle. Will he win the horse? What do you say?

5. Charny demande:

En l'emprise est dit que qui tue cheval de cop de lance, il le paiera. Si avient que au jouster li uns fiert le cheval de l'autre de sa lance bien avant; maiz ils hurtent de leurs chevaux si durement que li uns et li autre s'en vont par terre. Paiera le cheval cil qui le fert de lance ou non. Qu'en dictes vous?

6. Charny demande:

Chevaliers et escuiers joustent d'une emprise, la criee comme dessus. Uns chevaliers porte fors de la selle uns escuiers de cop de lance, ou un escuier un chevalier. Gaignera il le cheval? Qu'en dictes vous?

5. Charny asks:

In the emprise it is said that anyone who kills a horse with a stroke of a lance will pay for it. So it happens that in jousting one strikes the other's horse with his lance well advanced; but their horses collide so hard that both of them fall to the ground. Will he who struck the horse with the lance pay for it or not? What do you say?

6. Charny asks:

Knights and squires joust in an emprise, with the announced rules as above. One knight knocks a squire out of the saddle, or a squire does the same to a knight. Will he win the horse? What do you say?

7. Charny demande:

Une emprise de chevaliers ou d'escuiers se fait pour jouster ainsi criee comme dessus. Si avient que .j. de ceulx de dedanz si jouste a un de ceulx de dehors; et pour ce qu'il forcoroient cil de dehors giette sa lance et la lance au gietter fiert du bout derriere en terre. Et avant que li bout devant fust percheüz il fiert parmi le cheval de l'autre et le tue. Rendre cil de dehors le cheval? Qu'en dictes vous?

8. Charny demande:

Uns baneres dehors envoie de ses atours a pluseurs chevaliers pour issir avec lui es champs pour jouster a ceulx de l'emprise; cilz chevaliers lui octroient et saillent sur leurs chevaux mesmes qui sont leur. Si en y a .ij. ou .iij. qui ont leurs chevaux mors et afolez au jouster de hurtee ou de cheoite, sera le baneres tenuz a leur rendre? Qu'en dictes vous?

7. Charny asks:

An emprise is arranged for jousting of either knights or squires, with the announced rules as above. So it happens that one of the home team jousts in this way with one of the visitors, and because he was running out of bounds, the visitor throws his lance and the thrown lance strikes its butt end on the ground. And before the front end falls down it pierces the other's horse and kills it. Does the visitor give recompense for the horse? What do you say?

8. Charny asks:

A banneret sends out from his entourage some knights to go out with him in the fields to joust with those who have set the emprise; those knights agree with him and sally forth on their own horses which are with them. If there are two or three of them whose horses are dead and injured in the joust from blows or falls, will the banneret be obliged to compensate them? What do you say?

9. Charny demande:

Une emprise comme dessus: Avient que un dehors jouste a uns autres de dedanz; et celui dedanz fiert le cheval de celui de dehors de sa lance par la teste ou autre part et fu de premiers cours de celui de dehors. Si ne veult mie descendre tant qu'il ait couru ses .ii. lances qu'il a encore a courre; et quant il a couru il envoie le cheval a l'autre de dedanz, et li mande qu'il le rende. Le rendra il? Qu'en dictes vous?

10. Charny demande:

Une emprise comme dessus: Uns chevaux est ferus de cop de lance et celui qui est dessus descent en l'eure et l'envoie a son hostelet. Lendemain l'envoie a l'ostel de celui qui le fert. Le paiera il? Qu'en dictes vous?

9. Charny asks:

There is an emprise as above. It happens that one of the visitors jousts with one of the home team; and the home knight strikes the visitor's horse on the head or some other part, and it was the visitor's first course. So he does not wish to get down before he has run the two lances which he has yet to run; and when he has run them he sends the horse to the defender, and demands that he compensate him. Will he compensate him? What do you say?

10. Charny asks:

There is an emprise as above. A horse is struck by a lance and the one who is riding it dismounts right away and sends it to his inn. The next day he sends it to the inn of the man who struck it. Will he pay him? What do you say?

11. Charny demande:

Deux chevaliers joustent en l'emprise desssus et a l'assener des lances li uns et li autres vuide la selle. Devra chascun prendre le cheval de son compaignon, ou se chascun se tenra au sien? Qu'en dictes vous?

12. Charny demande:

Uns escuiers si s'embat tout armez pour jouster a une emprise de chevaliers et jouste; et un chevalier de l'emprise le porte hors de la sele de cop de lance. Gaaignera le chevalier le cheval, quar chascun cuidoit qu'il fust .i. chevaliers jusqu'a tant qu'il fust jus, mais doreure ne portoit il point. Qu'en sera il jugie par droit d'armes?

11. Charny asks:

Two knights joust in the contest described above and at the striking of the lances both come out of the saddle. Will each take the horse of his companion, or each be content with his own? What do you say?

12. Charny asks:

A squire, completely armed for jousting, enters an emprise for knights and jousts; and a knight of the emprise knocks him out of the saddle with the stroke of the lance. Will the knight win the horse, for each believed that he was a knight until he was down, but he did not wear any golden accouterments. How will it be judged according to the law of arms?

13. Charny demande:

Uns chevaliers si s'embat tout armez comme chevalier pour jouster a une emprise d'escuiers; et .j. escuier de l'emprise le porte hors de la sele de cop de lance. Gaaignera l'escuier le cheval? Qu'en dictes vous? Que li aucuns tiennent?

14. Charny demande:

Uns chevaliers de l'emprise fiert des esperons, et deux chevaliers dehors, chascun visant de sa lance, viennent contre lui. Et celui dedanz ataint de sa lance le premier des deux et le porte hors de sa sele; et li autres des deux ataint le chevalier de dedanz. Et de son cop mesmes celi dehors se porte hors de sa sele; et a celui cop celui dedanz n'avoit point de lance. Gaaignera celi dedanz les .ij. chevaux dehors? Qu'en dictes vous?

13. Charny asks:

A knight, armed as a knight, enters and jousts in an emprise for squires; and one squire in the emprise knocks him out of the saddle with a stroke of the lance. Will the squire win the horse? What do you say? What do others think?

14. Charny asks:

A knight of the emprise strikes his horse with his spurs, and two of the visiting knights, each one aiming with his lance, come against him. And the home knight hits the first of the two with his lance and knocks him out of the saddle, and the second strikes the home knight. And with the same blow, the visiting knight knocks himself out of the saddle; and at the time of the blow the home knight did not have a lance. Will the home knight win the two horses from the visitors? What do you say?

15. Charny demande:

Uns chevaliers de l'emprise fiert des esperons, visant de sa lance; et uns autres chevaliers dehors vient ferant de l'esperon a l'encontre de celui en ce meismes point. Si avient que li uns de ces deux aussi comme sur l'assigner fiert sa lance en terre, et de ce cop se porte a terre de la sele. Li autres gaignera il le cheval? Qu'en dictes vous, car il n'ont point assené l'un a l'autre?

16. Charny demande:

Uns chevaliers de l'emprise dessus dicte fiert des esperons, et de son premier cours il est blechié et se desarme; et en son harnois se met uns autres et monte sus son cheval pour jouster en lieu de celui qui est blechié, et par la volenté du blechié, combien qu'il n'estoit mie de l'emprise fors que pour aaidier aveques ceulx de l'emprise. Si jouste si bien que nulz de ceulx dedanz ni ataint de trop loing au dit de tous. Qui aura ce pris, ou celui qui a si bien jousté, ou son mestre pour qui il jousta, ou cil qui miex aura jousté apres li de ceulx de l'emprise? Qu'en dictes vous?

15. Charny asks:

A knight of the emprise strikes with his spurs, aiming with his lance, and another visiting knight comes striking with his spurs against him at the same time. So it happens that one of the two also as he is coming to strike him strikes his lance in the ground, and by this blow knocks himself out of the saddle and onto the ground. Will the other win his horse? What do you say, for the one has not struck the other?

16. Charny asks:

A knight of the emprise described above strikes his spurs and in his first course is wounded and disarms himself; and another puts on his harness and mounts his horse to joust in the place of him who was wounded with the agreement of the wounded man, even though he was not at all part of the emprise, but is only to aid those who had established the emprise. So he jousts so well that none of the home team in the judgment of all comes even close to him. Who will have the prize, he who jousted so well, or his master for whom he jousted, or whoever has jousted best among those holding the emprise after him? What do you say?

17. Charny demande:

Celui chevalier devant dit qui si bien a jousté pour son mestre, celui jour mesmes il fert .i. cheval de sa lance, lequel cheval lui fu envoié pour ce qu'il li rendist. Le rendra il, ou ses mestres? Qu'en dictes vous?

18. Charny demande:

Uns chevaliers jouste a la feste dessus a uns autres de cop de lance et le porte hors de la sele, fors tant que d'une de ses mains tient l'arçon de la sele avant qu'il soit du tout hors; mais plus ni demeure de lui que la main. Perdra il le cheval et sera gaaigné pour l'autre? Qu'en dictes vous?

17. Charny asks:

This aforesaid knight who has jousted so well for his master, that same day struck a horse with his lance, which horse was sent to him because he should have paid recompense for it. Will he pay recompense, or his master? What do you say?

18. Charny asks:

A knight who jousts at the above celebration has struck another with his lance and knocks him out of the saddle, except that with one of his hands he holds to the saddlebow, but otherwise he should be entirely out of the saddle; but no more of him remains on the saddle except his hand. Will he lose the horse and will the other win it? What do you say?

19. Charny demande:

Uns chevaliers ou uns escuiers a emprunté un cheval pour jouster a un autre compaignon et jouste sus; mais toutevoies vient l'hurter a son compaignon de cheval et de tout. Quant apres .iij. semaines ou .j. mois cil compaigns renvoit le cheval a celui de qui il avoit emprunté, le quelx chevaux n'avoit onques pris valu de la hurtee de chose que l'en y puist aparcevoir. Et li compaigns qui le presta le refuse a prendre pour cause de la hurtee, mais veult avoir le pris de cheval. Ainsi sont a debat. Qu'en dictes vous?

20. Charny demande:

Uns chevaliers porte un autre a terre a cop de lance ensemble son cheval, et li cheval ne se puet relever se le chevalier ne se oste de la sele. Se puet il oster de la sele sans congié de celui a qui il jouste? Et se il descent sanz congié de celui a qui il jouste et li cheval se relieve, cil qu'il le portera a terre, puet il demander le cheval par droit d'armes de joustes? Qu'en dictes vous?

19. Charny asks:

A knight or a squire has borrowed a horse for jousting from another companion and he jousts on; but nevertheless he happens to crash the horse into his companion's horse and equipment. When after three weeks or a month this companion returns the horse to the one from whom he borrowed it, that horse has not gained any value from the blows in any way that could be seen. And the companion who lent it refuses to take it, because of the blows, but wants to have the price of the horse. And so they are in contention. What do you say?

20. Charny asks:

A knight knocks another to the ground with a blow of his lance, and his horse with him, and the horse is not able to get up if the knight does not get out of the saddle. So is he able to get out of the saddle without the permission of the one he jousted with? And if he dismounts without the permission of him whom he jousted with, and the horse gets up, is he who knocked it to the ground able to claim the horse by the law of arms for jousting? What do you say?

[II. Tourneying]

Ce sont les demandes pour le tournoi que je Gyefroy de Charni fais a haut et puissant prince des Chevaliers Nostre Dame de la Noble Maison a estre jugiees par vous et les chevaliers de vostre noble compaignie.

1. Premierement je demande:

Si uns riches homs retient uns baneres, ou .j. baneres .i. chevalier pour certain fuer et pour la saison, ainsi sont acordez; et sur ce vienent a la ville ou le tournoy est crié et fait ou fenestres. Se li riches homs ou li banneres dessus vient hors sa baniere et sa retenue toute, uns autres riches homs fait parler a ce baneres ou chevalier dessus qu'ilz soient aveques lui pour l'annee; et li baneres li ottroie ou li baceler. Dont li riches homs qui a retenue pour l'annee fait lever le baneres qui es avecques l'autre et fait mettre hors a fenestres avecques lui. Se puet il faire par le droit d'armes de tournois? Qu'en dictes vous?

[II. Tourneying]

These are the questions concerning the tourney which I, Geoffroy de Charny, pose to the high and mighty prince of the Knights of Our Lady of the Noble House to be judged by you and the knights of your noble company.

First I ask:

So a rich man retains a banneret, or a banneret a knight, for a certain fee and for the season, and thus they are agreed; and afterwards they come to the city where the tourney has been proclaimed and arms displayed in the windows. So when the rich man or the banneret above comes without his banner and whole retinue, and another rich man speaks to the banneret or knight above, suggesting he should be with him for a year; and the banneret, or the knight takes the offer. Then the rich man who has retained him for a year goes to remove the banneret who is with the other and make him display his arms outside the windows with him. So is he able to do that by the law of arms for tourneys? What do you say?

2. Charny demande:

Se li riches homs qui celui baneres avoit retenu pour la saison et qui l'a perdu pour l'annee, s'il est dit ainsi, il refait parler a celi baneres qui est parti de li qu'il soit avecques lui a vie et le donne terre a sa vie tant qu'il sont acordez. Dont se li riches homs fait lever le baneres de la retenue du riche qui l'avoit retenu pour l'annee, et le fait mettre avecques lui comme devant. Li autre riche dit que non. Se puet il faire par le droit d'armes de tournois? Qu'en dictes vous?

3. Charni demande:

Si'l estoit dit qui se peust faire, et uns autres riches homs faisoit a celi baneres ou baceler proufit a heritage et le retenist, le pourroit il oster de cil qui l'a retenu a vie par le droit d'armes de tournois?

2. Charny asks:

So the rich man who had retained that banneret for a season and who has lost him for the year, if it is thus said, speaks again to the banneret who has left him, saying that the other should be retained for life and gives him land for life, as long as they are in agreement. So then the rich man goes to remove the banneret from the retinue of the rich man who had retained him for the year, and take him back with him as before. The other rich man says no. So can he do this by the law of arms for tourneys? What do you say?

3. Charny asks:

If it was said that he was able to do this, and another rich man gave to this banneret or bachelor a hereditary holding, and retained him, could the one who has retained him for life take him away by the law of arms for tourneys?

4. Charni demande:

Seroient pareilles retenues d'escuiers aussi comme il est dit des chevaliers dessus diz par le droit d'armes de tournois?

5. Charni demande:

Li disceur viennent prendre la foy de chevaliers en la maniere acoustumee et tuit la baillent fors que .j. baceler qui ne la veult bailler. Demourra a faire le tournoy par celi ou non par le droit d'armes de tournois?

4. Charny asks:

Are there the same contractual obligations for squires as is said above for knights by the law of arms for tourneys?

5. Charny asks:

The judges come to take the oath of the knights in the accustomed manner and all give it except one bachelor who is not willing to swear. Will he remain to take part in the tourney or not by the law of arms for tourneys?

6. Charni demande:

Se l'en ne laissoit pas a tournoier pour celui chevalier, et celui chevalier ne se vousist armer, et li disceur en faisoit crier le laiser et mettre les ataches es champs, et saillist on hors, et les routes faictes par les disceurs et leur dit quittié et assemblent. Et pluseurs sont qui sont tirez a terre et leurs chevaux emmenez. Et quant vient le soir cilz qui ont perdu leurs chevaux les demandent et dient que ce n'est mie tournoy. Qu'en sera il jugié par le droit d'armes de tournois?

7. Charni demande:

Li disceur font crier le lacier, les estaches mises es champs. Et quant tuit li chevalier sont es champs li disceur devisent le tournoy et aucunes des routes; et ycelles routes assemblent avant que il aient dit le tournoy es routes. Et avant qu'il puissent avoir dit le tournoy es derrenieres routes il vient chevaliers pluseurs de surcrois sur les champs; dont disceur ne pueent ordener plus avant qu'en celles routes. Les autres routes qui sont assemblees perdent et gaaignent chevaux et sont menez a l'estachete.

6. Charny asks:

So the judge did not allow this knight to tourney, and this knight did not wish to arm himself, and the judge had "tie it up" cried and had the cords [or stakes] put in the fields, and people went out and the troops were made by the judges and they say "you are released" to them, and they assemble. And there many are pulled to the ground and their horses are taken. And when the evening comes, those whose horses are lost ask for them back and say it was not a tourney at all. How will it be judged by the law of arms for tourneys?

7. Charny asks:

The judges have "tie it up" cried and the stakes put in the fields. And when all the knights are in the field the judges organize the tourney and some troops. And those troops assemble before they should have ordered the whole tourney into troops. And before they are able to order the tourney into the final troops there appear many more knights on the field; so the judges are not able to arrange any more of them into these troops. The other troops which are assembled lose and gain horses and are led to the stake. [Implied question: if the losers ask for their horses back and say that this was not a tourney at all, how will it be judged by the law of arms for tourneys?]

8. Charni demande:

Uns chevalier saut hors tout armez sanz couverture comme dessus pour tournoier sus .j. beau destrier. Et quant vient sur le chevauchier pour assembler celui chevalier monte sur .j. autre cheval. Et un desarmés monte sur le cheval dont il descendi et le tournoi durant li contens d'iceli chevalier et parsui celui cheval enmi les champs hors de toutes estachetes, sur quoi le chevalier sailli et descendi. Si prennent celui cheval et l'emmainent a leur estachete et boute jus le desarmé qui estoit sus et dient qu'il l'ont gaaigné. Le chevalier dit que non. Qu'en doit il estre par droit d'armes de tournois?

9. Charni demande:

Uns chevaliers tournoie avecques les autres comme dessus et tourne par acort; si est trait a terre et son cheval aussi. Cilz qu'ilz l'ont tiré a terre li font couper les sengles et le poitrail de la sele; et li cheval se lieve. Si l'emmainent a l'estachete; et li chevalier demeure a terre sa sele entre ses jambes. Est li cheval gaaignez ou perduz pour le chevalier? Qu'en diroit l'en par le droit d'armes de tournois?

8. Charny asks:

A knight sallies out all armed without any concealment as above to tourney on a beautiful destrier. And when he comes to ride it to the assembly point this knight mounts a different horse. And an unarmed man mounts the horse he has got down from and during the tourney with the agreement of this knight and pursues this horse in the middle of the fields outside all the stakes. So some others catch the horse and take it to their boundary of the field and knock down the unarmed man who was on it and they say that they have won it. The knight says no. How should it be according to the law of arms for tourneys?

9. Charny asks:

A knight tourneys with others as above and tourneys under mutually agreed rules; thus he is pulled to the ground and his horse, too. Those who have pulled him to the ground cut his girths and the breastplate of the saddle and the horse gets up. So they lead it to the stake and the knight remains on the ground with his saddle between his legs. Has the horse been won or lost by the knight? What will be said about it by the law of arms for tourneys?

10. Charni demande:

Uns escuiers ou deux ou trois armez pour le tournoi truevent un chevalier hors de merlees. Si l'arrestent et le tirent jus et emmainent le cheval a l'estachete. Quant vient le soir le chevalier demande son cheval pour ce qu'a son perdre il n'y ot nul chevalier. Li escuier dient que non. Qu'en sera il selonc le droit d'armes de tournoys?

11. Charni demande:

Un tournoi est fait par acort et tournoie l'en. Quant vient le soir bien tart l'en lieve les estachetes; mais puis grant piece demeurent plusieurs chevaliers sur les champs a la merlee et perdent et gaaignent chevaux assez et d'une part et d'autre. Et quant vient le soir plusieurs redemandent leurs chevaux qu'ilz perdirent puis que les estachetes furent levees. Qu'en sera il jugié par le droit d'armes de tournois?

10. Charny asks:

A squire or two or three armed for the tourney find a knight outside of the mêlée. So they stop him and pull him down and take the horse off to the stake. When evening comes the knight demands his horse because there was no knight present at his loss. The squires say no. What should happen according to the law of arms for tourneys?

11. Charny asks:

There is a tourney under mutually agreed rules and people are tourneying in it. When evening comes the stakes are taken up very late. But for a long time many knights remain on the field in a mêlée and they lose and win a number of horses on one side or the other. And when the evening comes many ask for the return of their horses because they lost them when the stakes were taken up. What will be judged in this case according to the law of arms for tourneys?

12. Charni demande:

Se aucun des chevaulx dessus demandez le soir estoit dit que l'en les rendist les aucuns, se l'en les attendoit a demander jusques a lendemain, leur seroit dit du rendre aussi bien comme s'il fussent demandes du soir?

13. Charni demande:

Uns tournois est fait par accort tout en une ville et sont mises les estachetes et crient le lacier et saillent hors. Et sur le point qu'ilz sont hors il vient .j. bacheler en la ville ou deux qui ne pueent avoir leurs chevax ne leur harnois celi jour. Et pour ce ne demeure il pas que les routes ne se facent et assemblent. Sera ce tournois ou non? Qu'en diries vous par le droit d'armes de tournois?

12. Charny asks:

If it was said, concerning any of the horses above demanded that evening, that some should be returned, if any others delay until the next day, should it be decided that those horses should be returned, as if they had asked in the evening?

13. Charny asks:

A tourney is arranged with mutually agreed rules in a city and the stakes are placed and "tie it up" is cried and they sally forth. And at the point where they are outside, one or two bachelors arrive in the city who are not able to have their horses or harness that day. And because of this they do not remain, nor do they join a troop nor assemble. Will this be a tournament or not? What will you say in this case by the laws of arms for tourneys?

14. Charni demande:

S'il sont entre .ij. villes et il avient ainsi comme dessus est dit, sera ce tournois ou tenuz pour encommensaille?

15. Charni demande:

Comment fait l'en un tournoy a estre dit tournoi et non autrement?

16. Charni demande:

Comment se fait encommensaille a estre dicte encommensaille et non autrement?

14. Charny asks:

If they are between two cities and it happens just as it is described above, will these be tourneying or held to take part in preliminary fights (encommensaille)?

15. Charny asks:

What is it that makes a tourney a tourney and not something else?

16. Charny asks:

What is it that makes a preliminary fight (encommensaille) a preliminary fight and not something else?

17. Charni demande:

Comment se font toupineures a estre dictes toupineures et non autrement?

18. Charni demande:

Le quel doit l'en miex prisier: ou celui qui pert deux chevaux ou .iij. en .j. jour bien ouvertement en assaillant ou en deffendant, ou celui qui tient son cheval tout le jour tout clos et bien enduré et sueffre le tirer et le ferir et tout ce qu'il li appartient? Qu'en dictes vous?

17. Charny asks:

What makes "toupineures" toupineures and not something else?

18. Charny asks:

Which is to be more highly prized: The one who loses two horses or three in one day while attacking or defending quite openly, or one who keeps his horse very close the whole day and endures and bears well the pulls and blows and everything that comes his way? What do you say?

19. Charni demande:

Uns baneres est au tournois et ses bacelers avecques lui de sa retenue; et faut l'en a tournoier en la semaine. Et aucuns des bacelers de ce baneres saillent aux commensailles et perdent leurs chevaux sanz congié de leur maistre, et sanz ce que leur maistre y ait esté. Quant vient au soir ilz demandent restour de leur chevaux; et leur maistre dit que non. Qu'en sera il jugié par le droit d'armes de tournois?

20. Charni demande:

Uns baneres vient en la semaine pour tournier et ne veult pas estre en son estat, mais se met dessoubs un autre comme .j. baceler. Aucuns compaignons sont en la ville qui sont de sa retenue pour l'annee, les quelx compaignons lui requierent qu'il leur face leur estouvoir, tant de monteurs comme d'autres choses. Leur maistre dit que non, pour ce qu'il ne veult pas estre en son estat; et le .ij. bachelers vont prendre leur proufit apres celle response pour l'annee avecques autres maistres. Li premier maistre dit qu'ilz ne le pueent faire; li bachelers dient que si font. Qu'en sera il jugié par le droit d'armes de tournois?

19. Charny asks:

A banneret is going to a tourney and has his bachelors with him in his retinue; and he wishes to tourney with it during the week. And some of the bachelors with him go out to the preliminary combats and lose their horses, without the permission of their master and without their master being there. When evening comes they request the return of their horses, and their master says no. How will it be judged by the law of arms for tourneys?

20. Charny asks:

A banneret comes during the week to tourney and does not wish to take part at his rank, but to take part under another as a bachelor. Also in the city are some companions who are retained by him for a year and these companions require him to give them their maintenance, both mounts and other things. Their master says no, because he does not wish to take that rank; and after this answer the two bachelors go to seek gain for a year with other masters. The first master says that they cannot do this. The bachelors say they can. How will it be judged by the law of arms for tourneys?

21. Charni demande:

Uns chevaliers et deux escuiers retenuz pour les tournois et pour l'annee. Le dit chevalier vient en la ville ou l'en doit tournoier hastivement et ne trueve pas ses escuiers et en retient deux autres la veille du tournoy. Et quant vint lendemain cilz deulx escuiers retenuz pour l'annee viennent avant eure de lacier et se presentent a leur maistre pour lui servir. Le maistre dit que non quant a la journee, quar pour icel jour il en a retenu deux autres. Dont li .ij. escuiers retenuz pour l'annee vont prendre leur proufit avecques autres maistres pour l'annee, et dient qu'ilz le pueent faire. Le premier maistre dit que non. Qu'en sera il jugié par droit d'armes de tournoys?

21. Charny asks:

A knight and two squires are contracted for the tourney and for the year. The knight hastily comes into the city where he wishes to tourney, doesn't find his squires, and retains two others on the eve of the tourney. And when the morning comes the two squires who are retained for a year come before the hour of "tie it up!" and present themselves to him ready to serve him. The master refuses them for the day, for this day he has retained two others. Then the two squires retained for a year go to seek their gain with other masters for a year, and say they are able to do it. The first master says no. What will be judged in this case by the law of arms for tourneys?

[III. War]
1. Premierement je demande:

Uns sires a tout son ost est devant une ville a siege; le quel seigneur a plusieurs chevetaines, et d'autres païs que du sien. Uns homs d'armes se part de l'ost, qui est a l'un des chevetaines dessus dit, et vient demander cop de lance a .i. des gens d'armes de la ville, le quel saut hors pour celi delivrer. Et a l'assembler li compains de la ville porte hors des arçons de cop de lance celui de l'ost et prent le cheval et l'emmaine en la ville; et ce fu fait au matin. Et ce jour mesme, quant vint au vespre uns autres compaigns de l'ost, et qui a .j. autre chevetaines que le premier n'estoit, va demander cop de lance a ceulx de la ville; et le compaigns de la ville, qui gaigna le cheval du matin, monte sur le cheval qu'il avoit gaaigné et vient hors pour delivrer le compaignon de l'ost. Si avient que le compaignon de l'ost porte a la terre celi de la ville et prent le cheval et l'emmaine en l'ost. Adont vient celi qui au matin avoit perdu le cheval et le demande comme sien; et cil qui a vespre l'a gaigné dit que non. Plusiers bonnes raisons y a dictes d'un coste et d'autre. Qu'en sera il jugié par droit d'armes?

[III. War]

1. First I ask:

A lord has his whole army before a city and is beseiging it, and that lord has many captains, and from other countries than his own. A man-at-arms who belongs to one of those captains leaves the army and goes to demand a stroke of the lance from one of the men-at-arms of the city, who sallies forth to deliver him. And having met him in combat, the companion from the city bears the one from the army out of the saddlebows with a stroke of the lance and takes the horse and leads it away into the city. And this was done in the morning. And that same day, when evening comes, another companion from the army, who belongs to a different captain than the first, goes to demand a stroke of the lance from those in the city. And the companion from the city who won the horse in the morning mounts the horse which he had won and goes out to deliver the companion from the army. So it happens that the companion of the army bears the one from the city to the earth and takes the horse and leads it away to the army. Then he who lost the horse in the morning comes and demands it back as his own; and the one who won it in the evening says no. Many good arguments are put forward about it on one side or the other. How will it be judged by the law of arms?

3. Charni demande:

Chevaliers joustent de fer de glaive par emprise; l'un porte l'autre de cop de lance. Gaignera le cheval celui qui aura porté l'autre a terre hors des arçons? Qu'en sera il jugié par droit d'armes?

4. Charni demande:

Assavoir se escuiers prendront autel droit comme chevaliers en tel cas.

5. Charni demande:

S'il estoit dit que li dessus dit peussent perdre ou gaignier, et .j. chevalier portast hors .j. escuier des arçons de fer de glaive. ou .j. escuier .j. chevalier, quel droit sera il du cheval, ou s'il ne sera ne perdu ne gaigné?

3. Charny asks:

Knights joust with steel lances in an emprise (under agreed-upon rules). One strikes the other with his lance. Will the one who will knock the other to the ground out of the saddle win the horse? How will it be judged by the law of arms?

4. Charny asks:

It is still to be decided whether squires will have the same rights as knights in such a case.

5. Charny asks:

If it was said that those mentioned above are able to lose or gain [horses], and a knight should knock an esquire out of the saddle with a steel lance, or an esquire a knight, what right will he have to the horse, or will it neither be lost nor gained?

Abbreviations for the Notes and Bibliography

Charny's *Questions Concerning the Joust, Tournaments, and War* are broken into the three sections indicated by the title. In this book I refer to individual questions by the section (J, T, or W) and by number. Thus, T14 = question 14 concerning tournaments. The full text of Charny's questions on jousting and tourneying and questions 1, 3, 4, and 5 on war can be found in Part II of this book, with an accompanying English translation. The text is taken from Michael Taylor's edition in his unpublished Ph.D. dissertation, University of North Carolina, 1977. My thanks to him for allowing excerpts from his edition to be included here. The translation is mine.

The translations from Froissart's *Chronicles* are based on Thomas Johnes' nineteenth-century version, which in some case have been corrected or modified to better conform to contemporary English usage.

Barber and Barker

Barber, Richard and Juliet Barker. *Tournaments: Jousts, chivalry and pageants in the Middle Ages*. Woodbridge: Boydell Press, 1989.

Barker

Barker, Juliet R.V. *The Tournament in England, 1100-1400*. Woodbridge: Boydell Press, 1986.

Fleckenstein

Fleckenstein, Josef, ed. *Das ritterliche Turnier im Mittelalter: Beiträge zu einer vergleichenden Formen- und Verhaltensgeschichte des Rittertums*. Göttingen: Vandenhoeck & Ruprecht, 1985.

Froissart

Froissart, Jean. *Oeuvres: Chroniques*. Edited by Kervyn de Lettenhove. 25 vols. in 26. Reprint edition. Osnabrück: Biblio Verlag, 1967.

Johnes

Froissart, Sir John. *Chronicles of England, France, Spain and the Adjoining Countries...* Translated by Thomas Johnes. 2 vols. London: Bohn, 1869.

René

King René's Tournament Book: René d'Anjou, Traictié de la forme et devis d'ung tournoy. Translated by Elizabeth Bennett. N.p., 1992. Online: http://www.princeton.edu/~ezb/rene/renehome.html

> For the French text of René I have used the version in Francis Henry Cripps-Day. *The History of the Tournament in England and France*. London: Bernard Quaritch, 1918. Appendix VIII.

Michael Anthony Taylor

Taylor, Michael Anthony, ed. "A Critical Edition of Geoffroy de Charny's 'Livre Charny' and the 'Demandes pour la joute, les tournois, et la guerre.'" Unpublished Ph.D. dissertation, University of North Carolina, 1977.

U.P.

University Press

Bibliography

This bibliography does not include works cited in the abbreviations.

Allmand, C.T., ed. *Society at War: The experience of England and France during the Hundred Years War.* New York: Barnes and Noble, 1973.

Anglo, Sydney. *The Great Tournament Roll of Westminster: A collotype reproduction of the manuscript.* Oxford: The Clarendon Press, 1968.

Ayton, Andrew. *Knights and Warhorses: Military service and the English aristocracy under Edward III.* Paperback ed. Woodbridge: Boydell Press, 1999.

Barker, Juliet and Maurice Keen. "The Medieval English Kings and the Tournament." In Fleckenstein, pp. 212-28.

Boulton, D'Arcy Jonathon Dacre. *The Knights of the Crown: The monarchical orders of knighthood in Later Medieval Europe 1325-1520.* Woodbridge: Boydell Press, 1987.

[Bretel, Jacques] Bretex ou Bretiaus, Jaques. *Le Tournoi de Chauvency.* Edited by Gaëtan Hecq. 2 volumes. Publications de la Société des Bibliophiles Belges séant à Mons, no. 31. Mons, 1898-1901.

Brush, Henry Raymond. "La Bataille de trente Anglois et de trente Bretons." *Modern Philology* 9(1911-2): 511-44; 10(1912-3): 82-136.

Christine de Pizan. *The Book of Deeds of Arms and of Chivalry.* Translated by Sumner Willard. Edited by Charity Cannon Willard. University Park, Pa.: Pennsylvania State U.P., 1999.

Contamine, Philippe. *Guerre, état et société à la fin du Moyen Âge: Études sur les armées des rois de France 1337-1494.* Paris: Mouton and EPHS, 1972.

—. "Les tournois en France à la fin du moyen âge." In Fleckenstein, pp. 425-449.

Coss, Peter. *The Knight in Medieval England, 1000-1400* (Coshohocken, Pa.: Combined Books, 1993).

—. "Knights, Esquires and the Origins of Social Gradation in England." *Transactions of the Royal Historical Society*, 6th series, 5(1995): pp. 155-178.

Cripps-Day, Francis Henry. *The History of the Tournament in England and France*. London: Bernard Quaritch, 1918.

Davis, R.H.C. "The Medieval Warhorse." In *Horses in European Economic History: A preliminary canter*, edited by F.M.L. Thompson. Reading: British Agricultural History Society, 1983. Pp. 4-20.

Dennys, Rodney. *The Heraldic Imagination*. London: Barrie & Jenkins, 1975.

Diaz de Gamez, Gutierre. *The Unconquered Knight: A chronicle of the deeds of Don Pero Niño, Count of Buelna*. Translated and selected by Joan Evans. London: Routledge, 1928.

Dyer, Christopher. *Standards of Living in the Later Middle Ages: Social change in England c. 1200-1520*. Cambridge: Cambridge U.P., 1989.

Gaucher, Elisabeth. "Les joutes de Saint-Inglevert: perception et écriture d'un événement historique pendant la guerre de Cent Ans." *Le Moyen Âge* 102(1996): 229-243.

Given-Wilson, Chris. *The English Nobility in the Late Middle Ages: The fourteenth-century political community*. London and New York: Routledge, 1987.

Jean Le Bel. *Le Chronique de Jean le Bel*. Edited by Jules Viard and Eugène Déprez. 2 vols. Paris: Librairie Renouard, 1904.

Keen, Maurice. *Chivalry*. New Haven and London: Yale U.P., 1984.

—. *The Laws of War in the Late Middle Ages*. London: Routledge and Kegan Paul, 1965.

—. "Heraldry and Hierarchy: Esquires and Gentlemen." In *Orders and Hierarchies in Late Medieval and Renaissance Europe*, edited by Jeffrey Denton. Toronto: University of Toronto Press, 1999. Pp. 94-108.

Kaeuper, Richard W. *Chivalry and Violence in Medieval Europe*. Oxford: Oxford U.P., 1999.

— and Elspeth Kennedy. *The Book of Chivalry of Geoffroi de Charny: Text, context, and translation*. University of Pennsylvania Press: Philadelphia, 1996.

Bibliography

Lopes, Fernão. *The English in Portugal, 1367-87: Extracts from the Chronicles of Dom Fernando and Dom João.* Translated by Derek W. Lomax and R.J. Oakley. Warminster: Aris and Phillips, 1988.

Meyer, Werner. "Turniergesellchaften: Bemerkungen zur sozialgeschichtlichen Bedeutung der Turniere im Spätmittelalter." In Fleckenstein, pp. 500-12.

Perroy, Edouard. "Social Mobility among the French Noblesse in the Later Middle Ages," *Past and Present* 21 (1962): 25-38.

Piaget, Arthur."Le Livre Messire Geoffroi de Charny," *Romania* 26(1897): 394-411.

Powicke, Michael. *Military Obligation in Medieval England : A study in liberty and duty.* Oxford: Clarendon Press, 1962.

Reynolds, Susan. *Kingdoms and Communities in Western Europe, 900-1300.* Oxford: Clarendon Press, 1984.

Roland, Ferdinand, ed. *Parties inédites de l'oeuvre de Sicilie, héraut d'Alphonse V roi d'Aragon, maréchal d'armes du pays de Hainaut, auteur du Blason des couleurs.* Publications de la Société des Bibliophiles des Belges séant à Mons, vol. 22. Mons, 1867.

Rösener, Werner. "Ritterliche Wirtschaftverhältnisse und Turnier im sozialen Wandel des Hochmittelalters." In Fleckenstein, pp. 296-338.

Rossbach, Jean, ed. "Les Demandes pour la joute, le tournoi, et la guerre de Geoffroi de Charny (XIVème siècle)." Unpublished dissertation, University of Brussels, 1961-2.

Rühl, Joachim K. "German Tournament Regulations of the 15th Century." *Journal of Sport History* 17 (1990): 163-82.

—. "Regulations for the Joust in Fifteenth-Century Europe: Francesco Sforza Visconti (1465) and John Tiptoft (1466)." *International Journal of the History of Sport,* 18(2001): 193-208.

Santina, Mary Arlene. *The Tournament and Literature: Literary representations of the medieval tournament in Old French works, 1150-1226.* New York: Peter Lang, 1999.

Strickland, Matthew. "Provoking or Avoiding Battle? Challenge, Duel, and Single Combat in Warfare of the High Middle Ages." In *Armies, Chivalry and Warfare in Medieval Britain and France,* edited by Matthew Strickland. Stamford, Lincolnshire: Paul Watkins Publishing, 1998. Pp. 317-343.

Sumption, Jonathon. *The Hundred Years War*. Vol. 1, *Trial by Battle*; Vol. 2, *Trial by Fire*. Philadelphia: University of Pennsylvania Press, 1990, 1999.

Taylor, Andrew. "Chivalric Conversation and the Denial of Male Fear." In *Conflicted Identities and Multiple Masculinities: Men in the Medieval West*, edited by Jacqueline Murray. New York and London: Garland Publishing, 1999. Pp. 169-188.

The Tree of Battles of Honoré Bonet. Edited and translated by G.W. Coopland Liverpool: Liverpool U.P., 1949.

Vale, Juliet. *Edward III and Chivalry: Chivalric society and its context 1270-1350*. Woodbridge: Boydell Press, 1982.

Van den Neste, Évelyne. *Tournois, joutes, pas d'armes dans les villes de Flandre a la fin du Moyen Age (1300-1486)*. Paris: École des Chartes, 1996.

Wyntoun, Androw of. *The Orygynale Cronykil of Scotland*. Edited by David Laing. 3 vols. Edinburgh: Edmonston and Douglas, 1872.

Chivalry Bookshelf

Publishers of New Works & Important Reprints
Western Martial Arts | Medieval History | Reenactment | Arms & Armour

Write for your free catalog or find us online:

http://www.chivalrybookshelf.com

4226 Cambridge Way
Union City, CA 94587 USA
866.268.1495 toll free | 510.471.2944 worldwide | 978.418.4774 fax